Living on Less & Loving It!

Penny Pinching With Style

Cathy Estabrook

Mobile, Alabama

Living on Less & Loving It!
by Cathy Estabrook
Copyright ©2016 Cathy Estabrook

Scripture is taken from the King James Version of the Bible. Public domain.

ISBN 978-1-58169-639-4
For Worldwide Distribution
Printed in the U.S.A.
Gazelle Press
P.O. Box 191540 • Mobile, AL 36619
800-367-8203

Table of Contents

1 How'd I Get Here? *1*

2 Mindset Matters *11*

3 Attainable Goals *16*

4 Savor Successes *19*

5 It Takes Time *22*

6 Back to Basics *28*

7 Monitoring Your Status *31*

8 Living Under Your Means *36*

9 Savings First *42*

10 Clever Cleaning *47*

11 Outdoor Oasis *51*

12 Creative Cooking *55*

13 Negotiate Naggers *61*

14 Shop Smart *64*

15 Crafty Cash *67*

16 Do the DIY *78*

17 Multiply Money *84*

18 Future Glance *93*

19 Mortgage Meltdown *100*

20 Got to Give *106*

21 Repurpose, Reuse, Rejoice *109*

22 Keep Climbing *111*

Acknowledgments

Thanks to my entire family Wade, Krystal, Wade Jr., Kerriann, and Valerie—without you this book wouldn't be possible. You are a gift from God that keeps giving. Love you all.

My Mom and Dad for all they have done.

Keith Carroll, my literary agent, for taking a chance on me and helping me to organize my thoughts.

Gazelle Press and Kathy Banashak, who was willing to take my words, polish them up, and present them to you.

Jodi Davies for sharing her peanut butter balls recipe years ago.

All you out there who share your experiences. We all learn from others.

Christian guidance I have received through the word of God and from other believers.

My close friends out there who endure my craziness and encourage me to dive deep.

Introduction

Do you live each week paycheck to paycheck, wishing something would change? Not sure what you would do if a serious incident occurred where you needed a lot of money or had to be out of work for a time?

I hear you and understand where you are coming from. That was my life for a long time after I turned seventeen. Through mistake after mistake and challenge upon challenge, slowly my life became transformed. This book will help you gain the security blanket you need to rest easy at night. I share some of the roads I have traveled down, which might seem familiar to you. I have also included many tips that are useful, have high impact, and some are downright fun! Discover super ways to put money in the bank and lessen the load in your life. Master the art of being a penny pincher with style.

1

How'd I Get Here?

For many of us who struggle in the financial grips of today's society, there are reasons why we are held captive. It's so important to understand why you are in the financial struggle you are in if you want to overcome it. Many of us have a crutch, a hardship, or a scapegoat explaining the reason we are sinking in the mad money pit. Some have had a tough beginning, some made poor choices, and others have had just plain harsh circumstances. Regardless of our reasoning, we need to decide it's time to make a positive change. Anything that requires change demands effort. Here's a taste of my situation:

There I was at the end of my junior year in high school planning the best year of my life, senior year! My plans went a bit awry, you might say. That summer I became pregnant and my boyfriend, Wade Estabrook, was only a sophomore in high school. The decisions we faced, the challenges that lay ahead, and the roads we would have to travel were daunting.

Neither one of us had a second thought about keeping the baby and raising that child the best we knew how and with the means we had available to us. But we were unsure of

1

what the next step would be. We were nervous, anxious, and didn't know where to turn. Not everyone agreed with our choices in life, but we took responsibility for them. It wasn't the beginning my husband nor I had anticipated.

Here I was only seventeen with a newborn baby and still in high school. My husband now, boyfriend then, Wade had just turned 16 and was only a sophomore in high school. At the time we lived in Stafford Springs, Connecticut. We looked high and low for an apartment we could afford but to no avail.

I managed to graduate from high school that year despite many migraines. Many of my friends disappeared quicker than a rabbit sinking in quicksand. My parents, a bit disappointed and shocked, looked upon our predicament with judgment and dismay. We felt alone and a little scared.

Wade had two years left of high school. What could we do? The only option we had was to pack our bags and move up North with my mother-in-law. When I say up North, I mean up North—to be more specific, the very last exit on Interstate 95 before you hit Canada—Houlton, Maine.

The move was essential for two main reasons. The first thought was we needed a place to live until we could get on our feet. The other huge piece was Wade needed to graduate and get out into the work force. Although the move was necessary, it was one of the hardest things I had ever experienced at the time.

I will never forget packing the bare minimum of my wardrobe, taking my baby, and jumping in a truck to travel eleven hours away from all I had ever known. My heart sank as I started driving away from my childhood home, all my belongings, and watching my parents and stepparents waving in the rearview mirror. My two brothers, parents, stepparents, and childhood friends were now going to be miles and miles away. I swallowed hard to keep back the tears. I knew I had to make the move, but it didn't ease the nervousness that settled in the bottom of my gut like a boulder falling into the sea. Not only was I leaving all my family behind, but I didn't even bring any of my belongings with me—not my cat or dog or even my bureau.

It's hard enough to raise a baby as a teenager, never mind without close family around. Wade and I had only been together for six months when I became pregnant. I really didn't even know his family well, and now I would be sharing a bathroom with them. I felt uncomfortable having to live with a family I knew so little about, but we had to make a go of it and this was the only way. I had to be strong, even though my knees were shaking and felt like jelly.

In life many times we find ourselves at crossroads. Each pathway has a different direction and many times alternate destinations. This was a big one for me! I had to go down a road I had never traveled and it wasn't going to be too pleasant of a journey. I knew it was the only option that would give us a chance.

Shortly after moving up to Houlton, we tied the knot with written permission from our parental units. We were too young otherwise. The wedding wasn't what I had ever pictured, but then again I was only a teenager so I hadn't

3

thought a lot about elaborate weddings. My future in-laws tried very hard to help, but really took over the planning of it. Since I was so young, I wasn't sure how to handle it. My family lived about 9 to 11 hours away, and I was on my own battling for any say in our wedding. The wedding had to be cheap and easy. We didn't have any money and I didn't have any family nearby.

We had to have relatives assist. My sister-in-law made the cake for us, the church we attended rented out a room in the basement of a Radio Shack for the reception, and our honeymoon consisted of driving down the highway a few hours and staying at a hotel on the northern coast of Maine, which was a gift from my mom. It wasn't a dreamy, classy wedding, but we loved each other and we were going to give it our best.

After the wedding we had to get serious about combatting the predicament we were in. Wade would be able to accomplish two years of high school in one due to the requirements in Maine. He worked with his brother-in-law after school. Graduation night is very vivid in my mind. I remember attending his safe Project Graduation all-nighter, knowing I was pregnant with our second child. That's right, he wasn't even out of high school and our second baby was on the way. We thought we were apprehensive before, but now we had two children for whom we would be responsible.

Things were moving along rapidly, and we weren't sure we would be able to keep our heads above water. When Wade won a mini-fridge at the all-nighter, we both were thrilled. First thing in the morning we brought the fridge back to the store for some quick cash. Any money was a help in our situation.

We were determined to prove to the world we could make it. We worked as diligently as beavers building a dam to take care of these children ourselves. When I say ourselves, I need to let you know God provided many times for us, but we worked and worked to make provision for our little ones.

We were also young and lived in the moment—both still teenagers with two little pumpkins to raise. It wasn't long and we were out on our own, living on pennies. I look back now and chuckle at some of the hardest times in our lives. I can vividly remember bathing the babies and then using the same bath water to scrub our clothes clean and hang them about the apartment. We had to pay for our water so it was pretty precious to us. Each of us probably have at least one of those clear memories of hard times, but Wade and I just had a few more due to the nature of our situation.

We rented a small apartment in the tiny town of Houlton, Maine. On a typical morning, Wade would rise and shine to milk cows on a dairy farm, head to work as a carpenter for eight hours, milk the cows again in the evening, and finally attend carpenter college for the ending of his day. His days were exhausting and his nights never seemed to settle down, but he was going to do what it took to make ends meet. Making enough money for rent, groceries, and heating the apartment was a chore. By some small miracle we made it.

One evening, near Christmas, my children and I were cuddled up on the couch and I was reading *Mickey Mouse's*

Christmas Carol to them. Our couch was so old and worn we had to set it on stacks of books because the legs were all broken off. The more I read, the more I noticed the similarities between Wade's boss, at the time, and Scrooge McDuck. Wade was an extremely hard worker and if given the opportunity would work from dawn to dusk. He was young, energetic, and felt like all he could do to help was work, work, work.

Back then if Wade worked more than forty hours, his boss gave him a day off instead of overtime. That made it difficult for us to earn extra money. However, in our minds we felt we needed to take care of our children, so we never received state assistance like food stamps, fuel assistance, or WIC. Granted we had a long road ahead but guess what? We made those choices, so as the saying goes, you made your bed now you need to lie in it. And that we did.

In our apartment, the heat never exceeded sixty degrees. My children had juice in their cereal many mornings because we didn't have the money to buy milk, but they survived. The kids and I sometimes giggle and talk about the juiced up cereal. The older two clearly remember those mornings. Despite all the financial hardships, we loved each other, and God was our rock. Hard work was all we knew and back then it would get us through.

At this point we pursued buying a house. Crazy, huh? Again we were only teenagers trying to purchase our first home. Oh boy, did the realtors snicker when they saw us coming in the door. But we had a burning desire to achieve. We not only looked unusual to the agents, but the loan officers at the bank found it strange we were looking to buy a house at our age. It was so bizarre that we needed to write a formal letter explaining why, at our age, we wanted a house.

We applied for a Maine State Housing loan so certain parts of the house needed attention before approval. I grabbed a tall ladder and started painting the trim around the three bedroom ranch. I'll never forget one day when I was painting, a relative popped by. She asked why I was doing all that work when I hadn't been approved for the loan yet. My response was simple, "Do you think God would bring me this far and not come through?" We became house owners as teenagers, woohoo!

Many trials and joys came over the next few years. And oh, I can't forget two more children! We took the scripture to be fruitful and multiply to heart (Genesis 1:28). Then my husband began working at a local mill (we had medical insurance for the first time) where he had a serious injury, sustaining the loss of three fingers down to his knuckle. Boy, did our lives change for a time.

Here we had four children and were only receiving two-thirds of our normal income. I might add we had to fight for a year to receive the appropriate amount. At this point in our lives, we didn't even own a credit card. Knowing where the money for weekly groceries would come from was a puzzle, and God was our puzzle solver. It was a very trying year and many hurdles were overcome through prayer. It brought me back to the apartment times all over again. We all endure setbacks and trials in life, but it's what we do with them that determines the outcome.

Eventually in 1998 I began attending a local university to achieve my Bachelor's Degree in Elementary Education. It was wild taking care of four little ones and hitting the books. My prayer life increased immensely to get me through. With perseverance and a big life change in December 2004, I graduated Cum Laude and began a teaching career.

Here's where we began to get a bit out of control with money. Up until this part of our lives, we lived extremely frugally. We had to; it meant survival for our family. But now we both had full time jobs. I obtained a few credit cards and oh did I start to use them!

I thought to myself, *How fun is this? Purchase what I would like and pay for it later. What a concept!* Each year I would rack up $12,000 to $18,000 worth of credit card bills. The rationale in my mind was, *Oh it doesn't matter; when we get our tax return, we'll pay it off.*

We never had any savings, and we continued to refinance our home to make improvements and build additions to the existing house. Our house started as a small three-bedroom, one-bathroom ranch. It now has a very large living room, another bathroom and bedroom, a sunroom, mudroom, shed, and a two car garage. These were drastic changes that were extremely costly. With all those additions, we more than doubled the amount we owed on the house.

Then as time passed, my oldest daughter, Krystal, graduated from high school and was going to go to Bible school in Canada, so she needed a vehicle or she would be stuck in a foreign country. We couldn't have that now, could we? On top of maxing out our home equity, we decided to buy a brand new vehicle we really couldn't afford.

Of course if you're sinking in debt already, just take one more dive down—living the American dream by suffocating in debt. By buying the new car, we could give my daughter our four-wheel drive truck. Here in northern Maine we have long, cold winters. The truck would keep her safe when traveling. This was my first kiddo heading off to college, and I wanted to make sure she was okay.

We were drowning in credit card debt, our house payment more than tripled, and now had a new vehicle payment. What was I going to do? Having a high mortgage, consumed with debt, and owning a new car was the norm, or so I thought. But I could no longer pay my bills! I went back to what I knew, the only thing I knew—hard work.

I picked up a second job so we could make ends meet. Eventually we paid off the car early and refinanced our home at 2.99% in a ten year term. I now have a three month emergency fund; I contribute to a Roth IRA, my savings, and a 401K. Not to mention, I am credit card debt free!

How did I get there? I want you to understand God is a big part of my success story! Currently our four children are living with us. Three are in college at a local university. One is engaged, getting married in six months, and a registered nurse. Please understand I am aware I still have a long way to go, but oh baby, I am not sinking like I was.

About five years ago, I slowly began to educate myself on money, budgeting, and retirement. In fact I still do on a constant basis. I have read many books and articles to learn ideas and strategies to dig out of the debt pit. Dave Ramsey is very knowledgeable and his work was extreme helpful to me. By writing this book I am hoping to help others gain financial knowledge to avoid the pitfalls society tells you are part of the "American Dream."

2

Mindset Matters

Can you think back to your younger years when you thought anything was possible? I remember, as a little girl, I truly thought if I could run fast enough I could become airborne. I can't even count the days I would go in the backyard and run like the wind, expecting to take flight. Of course with time comes experience and with experience comes knowledge. So I learned I did not have the ability to fly. But many times what we believe can happen will come to pass.

The way you view your finances is one of the most powerful tools in your toolbox. In recent years, I view spending my hard earned money completely different than I used to. Charging items for my kids, clothes for my family, and just racking up the plastic for what I thought we needed was easy, and I never gave it a second thought. If any of my children needed something for school, sports, or dance classes, I immediately ran out and charged it or found it online. There wasn't one moment of hesitation or one thought of the repercussions of my actions.

This behavior began to change when I started working my second job as a waitress. My hourly wage was $3.75 an hour. As mentioned earlier in the book, I reside in a small town, so sometimes the restaurant I work at is extremely busy and other times it's super slow.

The first few months of working there, I would go to clean off a table and sometimes find only a $2 tip. I thought *What will this help?* but as the night progressed those $2 tips added up. It was a huge aha moment as they say. If $2 can add up like this in one night, it can surely make a difference in my finances. It was a daily double. I also learned I was working quite hard for my money so I needed to be wiser with it. From that time on, I thought of saving money in a different light.

Generally I averaged about $14,000 in credit card debt yearly. I knew that we would be receiving a healthy tax return and I could just pay it off again. It didn't seem to faze me and I never lost any sleep over it. It was part of our economic lifestyle. We just figured we needed to provide for our children and be there for them. It was our responsibility. Yes, it is your parental responsibility to provide for your children, but does that include the most outrageously priced sneakers that everyone is wearing? Or sinking your family's financial ship in order to keep up with the neighbors? No, supporting your children does not encompass buying the very best that is ridiculously overpriced or making sure they're up to speed on every latest trend.

A drastic change in my thought process was looking at the items in terms of how long I would have to work to buy it. Even something as simple as your morning stop for coffee—take that quick stop and think about how long you'll be working to buy it. Take it a step further if you stop for coffee each workday and multiply that times five. That's how much money you're spending each week on just coffee. You could multiply that last number times fifty-two, and now you know how much you spend on morning coffee on a yearly basis.

When you look at purchases as equivalent hours of work, it totally changes your perspective. I used to use my credit card with ease, and now I reluctantly pull it out and quickly do some math in my head. If the items cost me $350, I think how that will take me x amount of hours to work before I can pay it off. Viewing purchases as hours worked shines a revealing light on the item in question. Automatically it discourages you from unnecessary purchases. It also helped me to realize the difference between wants and needs. In earlier years, I viewed many of my wants as needs. There is a huge difference between a want and need. We need love, food, clothing, and shelter. Those are needs. Top brand sneakers, fancy organic groceries, and a new vehicle are wants.

In my family, we always have plenty of food, thankfully, but much of it is generic brand. All of my baking supplies are generic. I use up what I have in my cupboards and freezer before I stock up again. When I write up my grocery list, I inspect my cabinets well and scour my refrigerator. My clothing can come anywhere from salvage stores like Marden's to great sales at JC Penney's. It all depends on where I will save the most money.

As of late I only buy footwear and clothing when I need them. I analyze whether I really need an item or if it is just a waste of money. Do I really want to work three hours to buy it? Do I truly need it? Just think about how long you will have to work for an item. Dig a little deeper and ask yourself do I really need it or will I really use it? Is it worth the labor I will have to invest?

I do not need the latest fashion with the biggest price tag and neither do my children! Frankly, I never cared what brand was on my tag, but boy, do my children. As parents we're out there working hard, budgeting every penny, and trying to keep everything going. It's okay to let your children know that $100 sneakers aren't doable right now but that you have $60 for them and together you'll look for the best deal. Let your children know you are on a budget, and a certain amount is what is allotted for each purchase.

There are better ways to achieve similar goals. One great way to teach children responsibility and lessen your load is to have your children earn a portion of the money needed. The child's age will determine what job is best for that child. A younger child should have to do a smaller amount of chores for some of the money.

Two things happen when you require your children to participate. Children learn that in order to buy or receive something they like, they need to work hard in order to contribute toward the purchase. The life lesson of working hard to obtain goods is almost a lost principle in society today. Another perk to doing this is that it will help you, as the parent, accomplish what you need to have done. If your child is older, he or she could babysit, deliver newspapers, or mow lawns in order to accumulate some extra money. It is so important for children to understand that it takes hard work to buy wanted items. Either way the child and the parent gain positive ground in sharing the load.

When my children started getting older, I would give them each a certain amount of money for school clothes. They would then have to decide if they wanted to buy an expensive brand of jeans or three pairs of jeans that are a third of the price. Let's be honest, will it really matter five years from now what brand of jeans you're wearing or what type of sweatshirt you have on today? Those material items do not matter. Society teaches you exactly the opposite, but when you meet someone new what is important is how you treat that person not what you were wearing when you met them.

Whether you have a great paying job or a minimum wage job, take a minute to pause and think about how hard you work. Each one of us in the workforce must clock in and get down to business. Take your hard earned cash seriously. Think about how long you will have to be punched in and slaving away for that purchase. Is there a better option or maybe do you really even need that item at all? Ponder the situation and then act. Our families and their needs are very important but so is stabilizing their future. Remember to stash some of your hard earned cash.

3

Attainable Goals

Who doesn't remember those soccer games when you were just a kid with one mission in mind? There I would be on a hot summer day fiercely running down the soccer field with determination and speed. I had only one thing in mind—a corner shot followed by a roar of the crowd. All I saw was the net ahead of me. The defenders and goalkeeper were minor obstructions that would not stop me.

Think back in your life to the days when you thought you could do anything and become whatever you set your mind to become. Once you have that thought etched, begin creating a pathway to that goal.

What is a goal and why do I need one? A goal is something one desires to accomplish. Goals are individual and need to be personalized by how you view your future. Where do you want to be financially in five years, in one year, or in six months? Goals create action for success and help us to persevere. They generate purpose and cause change.

It is so crucial to have a goal to strive for and a finish to obtain. Every person will work harder for a specific outcome. When you do not have a purpose or a reason for doing an activity, it's like a hamster running on a stationary wheel. You are going and going but aren't sure why you are doing it or where you are heading. Find a focal point and concentrate on getting there. Goals are necessary ingredients to a successful financial recipe.

Please take some time and think about what you would like to accomplish financially. Remember, when beginning this positive strive toward the finish line, take small, careful steps. Creating a goal that you are able to accomplish is self-motivating, encouraging, and helps you to strive on. It's like training for an event. You need to start small and work continually to complete your preparation. It's very encouraging to any individual to be able to say, "Hey, I did it!" Attaining a goal gives you more motivation, inspires you to continue on to bigger goals, and molds you into better financial shape.

One of the first things I did was to begin saving $1,000 for any house repairs or unexpected bills that might occur. At the time it was hard for me to even fathom having three to six months' worth of income as an emergency fund. I needed a smaller goal that I was able to achieve. When I began this journey, $1,000 in a bank account seemed really difficult and hard to obtain, but all the articles and books I read recommended this as being one of your first steps.

It is definitely a wise number one step, but when our paychecks were gone before they arrived, that $1,000 seemed nearly impossible. It seemed so far out of reach, but hear me, the more I looked at my budget and the more I trimmed where I could, researched how to save money, and started taking this challenge on, the quicker my situation began to improve. You need to decide what your goal is and begin feverishly pursuing it.

I always thought we needed to spend what we made, and I did not have any wiggle room to save any money. I felt thankful I could pay all our bills but forget saving anything. That was not the right mindset. You need to set an objective and persevere. It may take time to triumph over your first goal, but after that one is conquered, the next will seem a little easier. Looking at nature for inspiration, we need to have the work ethic of a squirrel preparing for winter. They keep scouring through the woods, gathering nuts, saving them for a later time, and then returning for more. Think of your money as the food stored for your family's future survival.

4

Savor Successes

When my four children were young, I felt rewards for hard work were important so they would learn that hard work brings great gains. Throughout the week they would have small chores, dependent on their age, that they would be required to accomplish. They didn't love the chores, but they sure appreciated the bonus at the end of the week, similar to many of us. We may not enjoy getting up at 5:30 am each weekday morning, but we appreciate the paycheck derived from it.

When the incentives were put into play, the eagerness and excitement were evident. They knew that at the end of their chore week, there was a payday worth the effort they put forth. Human nature is just so. Positive external reinforcement helps to create an internal drive. They became just like the seven dwarfs, "Hi ho, hi ho, it's off to chores we go."

I made colorful tickets that would contain one of three choices: movie and popcorn Friday night, sundaes on Saturdays, or Friday night pizza. There were smiles ear to ear when I would take the tickets off the fridge on Thursday night and offer them to the kids. The littler ones would be jumping up and down just waiting for me to take them down from high off the fridge and out of their reach. What used to be a goal too high to grasp was now heading in their direction. As I am writing this, a grin comes to my face recalling the sparkle in their eyes attained by their accomplishments. They were so proud of themselves for doing a good job and receiving a prize. It wasn't a huge gift, but it meant a ton to those kiddos.

When you are working hard all week at saving money, taking care of your family, and working outside the home, you too need a reward for yourself. It's so vital to first look at what you have accomplished thus far. Each little stash of money you accumulate deserves a high five! I know I've been there, and it takes determination and consistency to do it. Take a minute to celebrate what you have done. It's not easy to change your life or your mindset. This is a process and for each step you climb up, stop and rejoice. Thank God for what has been done and thank Him for your future endeavors.

The next part is equally significant and that is to make sure you treat yourself in some small way. Realizing that the objective of reading this book is to incorporate savings and change in your life, you need to give yourself a little break, whether that is going out to eat every two weeks with your husband, going to the movies with your family, or going bowling with a group of friends.

If you are in dire straits with your finances, be creative with ideas that do not take money. For example, instead of going out to eat, gather a basketful of tasty picnic foods and head off with your husband to a scenic spot you both enjoy.

Have a movie night at one of your girlfriend's houses. Have a big game night at your house and invite a bunch of couples and ask all the guests to bring some food to share. It's like a fun night buffet. Just remember to reward your efforts in some positive way.

You need to let yourself have a little fun. All work and no play can make stashing money go away. In other words if you are hyper-focused on saving money and budgeting, you will exert all your energy into this cause and eventually burn out. Taking a well-deserved break every two weeks or even monthly will allow you to have a respite and then in turn be ready to conquer the next money goal. Letting yourself relax, have fun, and reap the hard work harvest is more profitable than constantly going full bore ahead and crashing.

Think about what you really enjoy. Once you have a prioritized list, start going down it every two weeks. It will keep you engaged on your saving journey, and most of all, it will encourage you to keep going. We need incentives to keep up a good job. Moreover seeing the gain and rewarding the successes give you momentum. Sometimes our dreams seem out of reach but breaking them down to small reachable goals make them seem easier to obtain. Each step is worth celebrating.

5

It Takes Time

The day I ventured into the Houlton Outreach Center to enroll in the University of Maine at Presque Isle, I knew I had a long road ahead with many challenges. I had four small children ranging in age from my youngest daughter who was two to my oldest daughter who was eight. It would be difficult attending college and tending to my four small children at the same time. With my youngest by my side, I walked in the office of the center's advisor and told her I wanted to take a full course load so in two years I would have my Associate's Degree. She took a few minutes to get to know my situation and where I was in life. Knowing about my little ones and how my husband was still working two jobs, she felt five classes might be a bit too much for me to swallow at the time.

She graciously suggested for me to start off a bit slower. Honestly, I wasn't too pleased with what she had said. I had a plan and it consisted of attending college full time, graduating in four years, and joining the full time work force. Her advice of taking only three courses a semester was not what I had in mind; for that matter, I didn't even see it as an option, but she was absolutely right. It was quite an adjustment to hit the books. Juggling the children's activities, church, meal-times, housework, shopping, paying bills etc. I would have started dropping all the balls of life I was juggling if I had taken five classes at the time. Each part of my life would have started crumbling.

During this time, I waited to do any homework until I had read to the children and tucked them in bed. This way I didn't take any more time away from them. I felt like leaving them to attend class was enough for them to adjust to. This left me working into the wee hours of the night and some-times into the next morning to finish my homework. As time ticked on, I began taking more classes, but it was a slow process. However, I was always moving forward toward my goal of graduating. Anything that is of value takes time to achieve.

Please understand it also takes time to dig out of a finan-cial pit. As you have seen in the first chapter, most of my life our finances have been strained, and we have barely squeaked by. It wasn't until about six years ago when I put my work gloves on, began stashing money where I could, and started working two jobs that things really began to change. Nothing worth doing is done overnight. Here I am six years later turning around my finances, although I still have much to learn and many habits to overcome. By no means am I rich, nor do I have the ability to retire early, but there is light at the end of my financial future.

I started by putting one foot in front of the other. It doesn't matter who you are, where you have been, or where you are now, it matters how determined you are to achieve your aspirations. Your attitude, willingness to learn, and work ethic can change a continuous battle into a victorious win.

There will be times in this voyage when you will feel like turning back because it would be easier to live the way you were living for so long. Yes it is easier to pull out that credit card, charge what you want, and enjoy the goods. Unfortunately that shopping exhilaration only lasts for thirty days until it comes time to pay the piper. It's also effortless to grocery shop by just throwing whatever you want in the cart; I did that for years. I thought to myself *We may not have much but by golly we are going to eat well.* So I would spend an abundance of money on groceries, although it does take a lot of money to feed six mouths.

What needs to be learned is there is a balance and ways to save money when grocery shopping. Making all my own cleaning supplies and detergent saves me a load of money, but it is a tremendous effort on my behalf and is probably not for everyone. But there are things every family can do to save money. Laziness has no place in this journey. It takes minimal effort to unscrew a bottle of liquid detergent and pour it into the washer. In contrast, shaving twelve bars of soap requires time and much exertion. Even some of my family members' mouths will drop when I talk about all the DIY products I make. Countless amounts of people just plain won't put in this much labor and time. But I am here to say it works. Life is full of choices. It's your decision to make a change today in order to live better tomorrow.

Ask yourself how badly you want to be financially stable. I know for me I was so tired of living paycheck to paycheck and praying to God that nothing would happen. I still do pray and ask God to keep all of us, but we are in better financial shape than we have ever been in.

I do credit God for everything good in my life and helping continuously in our lives. God is the reason we, as teenagers, were able to feed, clothe, and provide a home for our children, without a doubt! My gratitude I have for Jesus intervening in my life and my family's lives is never ending. Nor could I ever repay God for all He has done for my family and me.

Faith is so significant. "Faith is the substance of things hoped for the evidence of things not seen" (Heb. 11:1). You need to have hope. I am a true dreamer and someone who believes the impossible is possible. I have seen so many miracles and experienced dreams that have become a realities. In Jesus's words, "If thou canst believe, all things are possible to him that believeth" (Mark 9:23). Believe it will get better, and rely on God to lead you in the pathway. When you take the steps necessary to help your family, God is there to help but wants us to walk right alongside of Him. Rely on Him for strength, wisdom, and direction.

Leaning on family and friends is another recipe for success. First of all, your family is your team and you need to work together. Having a family meeting to help everyone understand your goals and plan of attack is a great first step. There will be adjustments made on everyone's behalf. When you trim the budget, lessen the entertainment, and shop wisely, the spending habits of the family as a whole will need to transform. This is difficult, and if your children are older, it will probably be even harder, but you need to make the changes.

For instance, if my son refuses to use my homemade laundry detergent, then he has to buy his own. He works and if he would rather spend money on detergent than use mine, it's his loss. Remember it will take a bit of time for the family to adjust to the drastic financial transformation you are imposing upon them. My family still comments on my electricity policing. I am constantly shutting off lights, power strips etc. The good news is that they finally do begin to accept the concept and will even embrace some of the ideas themselves. It will probably not be an overnight acceptance but rather a slow tolerance of the changes. Teamwork will help you become triumphant in the end.

Friends are great supports and can really lend a hand. Again cluing them in to what you are trying to achieve is essential for a couple of reasons. For one, if your friends understands you are running a tight budget and are cutting back on going out to eat, they will not invite you to the most expensive restaurant but rather a more affordable one because of what you are trying to accomplish. They will respect your decision to gain financial stability for your family. Having them over for a potluck supper can work great too, and you're not losing out on quality time with them.

A friend can be a super person with whom to discuss your ideas. One of my friends, who lives right down the street, always give me terrific ideas and solutions for my problems. She is one of the best sounding boards I have. She gives me smart suggestions and is there for me. If I am under pressure, talking it out with her gives me much needed relief. Rely on those true friends; they'll be a wonderful support. We all need someone to talk to and someone we know is there for us.

Let's review. My husband and I got married when we were so young that we needed written permission to tie the knot. We had three of our four children by the time he was 19 and I was 20. Here we are 24 years later and still married. Now that doesn't mean we haven't traveled down some truly rough roads, but hey, we made it this far. In today's society that is unusual.

God kept us going. "For I am convinced that neither death, nor life, nor angels, nor principalities, nor things present, nor things to come, nor powers, nor height, nor depth, nor any other created thing, will be able to separate us from the love of God, which is in Christ Jesus our Lord" (Rom. 8:1). Have confidence in this, God loves you and can help you.

6

Back to Basics

My grandmother was an energetic, adventurous, story filled lady. It didn't matter where we were or what type of audience she had, she always shared a great story that captivated us all. She had a way of gaining everyone's attention and sustaining it. It was natural for her. She was an only child and had experienced so much. Each story had a small moral or humorous lesson learned.

We would be settled down and relaxing after a tasty family dinner in the comfort of a cozy living room when the words would start flowing. She would first grab us with an exciting quest she had been on. Her elaboration and details kept our attention while we waiting to see where this tale would take us. She had lived so big and traveled to places I had only dreamed of. I was like a sponge, soaking in the account that never had a dull ending. She was a walking memoir. The lessons I learned and the visions she had created for me are etched in my memory.

Sometimes the good old ways and the wisdom of those who have gone before can hold our answers. Woven through her stories were little old wise tales. History is one of the greatest teachers. What worked for struggling people years ago can work today too. Don't discount the successes of the past. Historically, America has survived many stressful economic times. Many attributes contributed to people's survival, but one of them is going back to the basics and spending less.

What you, as the financial captain of your ship, need to remember is you can save more by spending less. A little later on you will be exposed to what helped me save the most in the chapter titled, "Savings First." I had tried many things in order to save money, but none of them seemed to put any money in the bank. The more I researched, read testimonials, and listened to financial advice, the more I found ways to cut corners, slash my budget, and save money.

I have been working two jobs for almost seven years, but it wasn't until five years ago that I started to make any financial headway in my life. The more money we made, the more money we spent. We were part of the cycle of living paycheck to paycheck. Almost everyone I knew was living paycheck to paycheck so hey, that's life, right? Not if you're trying to be a penny pinching mother. We were paying our bills, able to buy groceries, and heat our home. We weren't ready for any type of emergency regardless of what it might be. In our minds that's why we had credit cards. On the contrary, I needed to learn to spend less and save more.

It's so vital to take time from your busy schedule and create a plan of attack on your finances. Sitting down to make a budget is necessary in order to have some wiggle room. Take every bill you have to pay even if it billed to you on a six month basis, like insurance, or a yearly basis like property taxes. Divide the six month bill by six and the yearly bill by twelve to determine what you will need monthly to meet all of your debits. Along with these bills add how much you spend on groceries and gas on a monthly basis. Don't forget any entertainment or charities you support too.

This is the amount of funds that leave your home monthly. Now see what you are paid on a monthly basis. The difference between the two is what you need to be automatically saving. If you are paid weekly, divide the difference by four. If you are paid bi-weekly divide it by two. Keep in mind you need to increase that saving as much as you can as time goes by. It comes down to living below your means, which I will go into with more detail in another chapter.

Now if you do not have a difference between the money leaving your house (bills) and the money coming into your house (paycheck), you need to make adjustments. It's imperative that you have less money going out of your house than the money coming in your household. That's where you need to apply some or all of the strategies that will be mentioned in this book. If you do not change your money management skills, your situation will not change, and you will stay stuck running in the game of life and not going anywhere.

7

Monitoring Your Status

I've always called my mom my Medical Mom. She was a registered nurse for years and has recently retired. She has much medical knowledge and was great in that field. I have asked her numerous times for advice on what to do when my children were sick or injured. Sometimes that call may have been made in the middle of the night, but that's the price you have to pay when you're the expert.

My mom was diagnosed with type two diabetes a few years back. Since that time she has to check her blood sugar levels each night for a couple of reasons. One of the most important reasons is to make sure her blood sugar level is within normal range. If it is not, she is able to take measures to combat the off balanced levels. In turn avoiding any further problems. Another vital point is regularly checking her glucose can prevent long-term complications that could occur and harmfully affect her health. Our finances are similar. If we do not check on them routinely, we could have severe future upsets or even current issues we are unaware of.

Understanding different aspects of your financial status is a serious responsibility. For example, retrieving an annual credit report should become routine. Going to www.annual-creditreport.com is a great website to obtain a report and print it out. On this site there are three places where you can get a free report. You are allowed to get one report from each place annually. My suggestion is to divide the three free reports you are allotted into the year. Print one out each quarter.

It is necessary to check your credit report to make sure there isn't any suspicious activity and to see for yourself what your credit looks like. Depending on your loan and credit card history, the report could be very lengthy. The first time you print out your report, it looks a bit confusing but if you read the introduction and look at what each code represents, it's not hard to understand at all.

Take the time to go through each individual entry on the report. Just recently when I printed my annual report, I noticed I had a credit card through one of my banks that I did not even open. So I called my bank right away and asked why it was available and then had them discontinue the card. Knowing what is listed under your credit report is so essential. This will help you to notice any activity that could be linked to identity theft. Also it will show you any activity that could be mistakenly placed under your social security number and name. The more you know, the stronger you are financially.

Do you have that irritating relative who always brings the conversation about to ask if you're sure you're ready for what's next? Have you planned ahead? Are your ducks in row? It just keeps going and going. They're like the energizer battery bunny except they're traveling down an annoying alley. Although they are always throwing at you what might be, possibilities, future heartaches etc., they have a valid point just not a good delivery. It's never too early to financially plan for the future or retirement.

Creating a social security online account or checking into a state retirement is another step in monitoring where you are. It doesn't matter if you are 25 or even 35 years away from retiring, you still need to have the knowledge of what you will be receiving. As I mentioned beforehand, I have paid into the social security system and into the Maine State Retirement System and continue to do so. There are a lot of rules and regulations in the state of Maine pertaining to what I am allowed to have regardless of what I have paid into the two systems. Maine is a beautiful state to live in, but for teachers it is not the best state to have worked in.

I started looking into my retirement about three or four years ago, even though I had 24 to 25 more years to work, and I am so glad I did. Due to all the regulations Maine bestows upon teachers, I have to plan extra hard to make sure retirement is possible without devastating consequences. When you are young and even middle aged, it seems like retirement is decades and decades away, but it creeps up quicker than we all would like to think.

When retrieving this information, it is critical to have the information on paper. What do I mean by this? When you talk to an employee at the social security administration, he or she may tell you one thing, but quite honestly if he or she cannot submit that on paper to you, chances are it is not so.

Getting your information on paper is imperative, and this way you have proof of what is yours. When looking into your future income, you need to be thorough and you need a paper trail. As daunting and tedious as it is, reading through all of the rules for the social security administration, other types of retirement, or state retirement is key to truly understanding what you are eligible for in the future.

As I read through pages and pages of information pertaining to teachers who work under the SSA as well contributing to Maine State Retirement, my mouth just dropped further and further down. I was absolutely astounded to learn how much retirement trouble I was in. I know you have heard this over and over again, but knowledge is power. Getting my future income in check was imperative. I needed to act right away so in the future I will be prepared and ready to retire. Know what you are looking at for income in your retirement years.

It is smart to have a ballpark figure of what you will be getting monthly from the jobs you have worked. The earlier you have an estimate, the quicker you have a base from which to work. You can then start supplementing for the future so you can maintain a similar lifestyle. Maintaining your current lifestyle is something else to ponder. You are now making more money than you will receive from social security or a state retirement. Just understanding what it will take to maintain your lifestyle in retirement is a journey in itself. You need to factor in inflation, cost of living, and having less income. There are formulas out there to help you adjust what you need, but I say it's good to overestimate. You never know what the future holds.

As you gain more financial ground and start investing wisely, it is necessary to monitor those investments as well. I have created online accounts for all our investments so I can monitor them monthly. Along with monitoring the accounts I record how each account is doing.

Please do not panic if you are young or even middle aged and see some losses when there is negative global activity. A prime example was when Ebola was spreading rapidly and beginning to alarm the world. The stock market started in a downward direction. Thankfully it was short-lived, but when watching your stocks monthly, it sure can make you nervous seeing your money dwindle. When you are young and even middle aged you have some time. Do not panic but steadily add to your accounts.

When you first begin keeping tabs on your financial growth and status, it will seem like a daunting task. But the more you do it, the easier and more routine it will become. Part of being a savvy saver constitutes knowing how much savings is needed for future endeavors. I mean, seriously, which one of us doesn't want to retire early? Retiring early requires much saving and serious planning.

8

Living Under Your Means

Years ago when my children were little, I wanted to make some outdoor memories with them. The kids and I went on a shopping spree late in the summer that year and Kmart had an awesome deal on a small above ground pool. Now an important aspect of this particular pool was that it needed to be set up on level, compact ground. Otherwise it would collapse and you would lose all the water. Keep that fact in the back of your mind as I share this story that created teardrops then but now generates giggles and chuckles.

Early one morning I began the construction of this "easy setup pool." I lugged dirt up in a wheelbarrow from the garden and began to level the ground off. About two hours into the job, my friend Janna joined me. She was foolish enough to volunteer to help me set it up. Wheelbarrow after wheelbarrow, we kept the dirt coming. It was a hot, humid summer day. The sweat seemed to run down our faces like rain down the gutter. We worked almost all day long, stopping only to feed the kids breakfast and then lunch. It was such a muggy day that is not seen often up this far north, but she was a trooper. I was determined to get it done, and she was a true friend to stick with me until the end. Shovelful after shovelful, wheelbarrow after wheelbarrow, we finally had what we thought would be enough.

Later that afternoon the ground looked ready and we were able to start setting up the pool. So we precisely placed the pool and began filling it up. It took quite a while to get the water at the right level, but as it was filling, it seemed to be working. Near the fill line we noticed the pool looked a little slanted but not too badly. The real test was to come when the four little ones would hit the pool. When they did, everything seemed okay initially. They were having a blast swimming and splashing, and laughter could be heard houses away.

So Janna and I decided to get some ice tea, sit on the deck in the late afternoon sun, and watch the kids play in the pool. We were both pretty proud of our accomplishment, although I have to admit we were exhausted from all the digging and lugging. We had worked all day long in the sun and heat and were ready for a rest.

Suddenly there was a loud noise and the gasp of four kiddos. The pool collapsed on one side and the water went gushing down the hill in the backyard. It sounded like a dam had just let loose. I couldn't believe my eyes! All the hard work, all that time, and all the money I had spent (well, technically charged) seemed like it went for nothing. The kids were astonished and upset all at the same time. I was distraught and dismayed. By the time my husband came home, I was in tears. My frustration level was through the roof. Thankfully he told me on the weekend he would fix it for us. And that he did.

You might be thinking, okay where is she going with this? A lopsided budget is like my off kilter pool—it just won't hold up. It is so important to make sure you have a smart budget but not just any budget. It must be a budget that has more money coming into your house compared to what is going out of your house. If you do not do this, your finances will go downhill just as quickly as the water that surged from my pool. Take it from me, it's not a pretty sight watching all that time and effort race downhill like Jeff Gordon down the track!

Regardless of your income, a budget must be formulated and you must live below your means. First determine how much income is coming into your household. Next write down every bit of money that goes out of your house each month. Make sure to include gas, groceries, entertainment, and every monthly bill you have. You will not be able to go forward until you have calculated your budget so that less money is going out then what is coming in. This is why tips on how to save money are so vital.

About five years ago, I sat down and created a monthly budget for my household. That was a great step but my budget was exactly equalized, meaning the amount of money coming in matched the amount of money going out for monthly expenses. I had a serious problem, and it wasn't going to get any better soon.

I slowly started going through the internet to find articles and books on how I could change what I was doing. At that point in my life, I was already working two jobs, and I was pretty sure working a third one wouldn't be feasible. That's when I stumbled across ways to save money. As I began to implement these money saving techniques I was able to slowly start saving money.

One thing that is really important is take the money you are saving and begin setting it aside. It is so easy to let the money that is being saved be absorbed into another area of outgoing money. The money being saved will surely add up, but it is not in huge increments.

For example, I started making my own detergents and cleaners. That saves me about $30 a month, so I needed to start putting that money in a savings account monthly. I continued to do this with all the other money savings tips that are mentioned in this book. After quite a while, I was able to set a certain amount of my paycheck automatically in my savings. It took me a long time to arrive at this stage. Just continue to make consistent strides and be determined to continue.

There will be strategies that do save you quite a bit of money, such as when I took my paid off car along with my son's car and changed the insurance coverage to just liability compared to full coverage. That little maneuver saved me $100 a month. Now that is quite a difference. It's terrific when you find a saving maneuver that is ongoing, but the key is to be smart with the savings. It's so easy to let the money go elsewhere.

A lot of my research offered many fantastic ideas, but some of these people weren't really living in the world I was living in. I have never been a person that has possessed a ton of money and material items and then lost everything. We never had too much to lose and have had to work very hard for what we do possess. Throughout my hours and hours of research, I never found a book that gave me upfront, manageable ways to change my life positively. I would scour the bookstores over and over again, check the magazine racks, and read and read. Not one book gave me ideas I could apply immediately to make a difference.

Most of my ideas and thoughts came from my experiences or experiences of others that I read about online. I am not discounting the wonderful books written to help those struggling financially because I have read them and used them. I just needed practical ways for a hard working country bumpkin like myself to balance my budget, making the money leaving my house less and the money coming into my house more; hence enabling me to save money for the first time in my adult life. The money saving moves this mother is going to share are unique and require some grit. A deep work ethic with an unwavering mindset are a must to have to be successful with this financial revolution.

My life has been comprised of financial struggle due to the choices I have made. My husband and I have always felt our family was our responsibility, notwithstanding the fact that we had three children when we were still teenagers. We never sought for outside help but felt we needed to take care of what is ours. We have worked very hard and tried the best we knew at the time. With saying all of that, I need you to understand that God has given us the strength to work hard, the wisdom to make a little travel go a long way, and to help us even when we made poor choices. Above all God has helped my family more than I could express or would take more time than I have to put into writing. God knows the hardships you are enduring; He loves you and will help you if you begin relying upon Him. "Casting all your cares upon him; for he careth for you" (1 Peter 5:7).

If you walk away with anything from this book take this motto with you: *Live Below Your Means.* Regardless of your income, it is imperative you make sure you are living well below your means. It's the only way to start putting pennies in your pocketbook and dollars in the bank. Now I do understand with a higher salary it is much easier to live below your means, but if you are like me, a higher salary does not describe my situation. Maine is one of the lowest paying states for teaching. With four children, living below my means came pretty hard especially in the financial hole in which we had fallen. That's why the money saving tips were vital in helping me start depositing coin after coin and make some noticeable changes.

It took me awhile to see the differences. I always just wanted to find that dream job with great pay, super benefits, and located in this one horse town. I still haven't found such a job, but that doesn't mean I was going to give up or lose ground. Decide to make some positive changes. If you continue you will see your dim financial situation begin to lighten up. The longer you apply these changes, the brighter your financial future will become.

9

Savings First

Who doesn't recall the saying, "A penny saved is a penny earned," by Benjamin Franklin? When I was young, I saved every bit of money I was given or earned. If I was given twenty dollars for my birthday, I would spend only a few dollars and save the rest of it. My saving account as a child was pretty impressive. I began babysitting when I was only eleven. Some of those jobs consisted of overnight jobs.

On one of my first overnight babysitting jobs, I was more than nervous. I put on a strong face, but the minute the parents left, I counted how many actual hours I would have to be responsible for these two children. We had a good evening and were rounding the corner toward nightfall., but I wished I never volunteered to watch these kids for the whole day and through the night. The children were very well behaved, but it was a huge responsibility for someone twelve years old.

We were outside after eating dinner, getting some fresh air before it was time to settle down for the night. The family had a nice swing set, so I was pushing the kids back and forth, dwelling on how much longer I had to go. I was getting more and more apprehensive about babysitting for the whole night. Unexpectedly my father pulled up. I had never been so relieved! Another adult was on the scene so I could relax for a moment or two. On top of coming and checking up on us, he showed up with ice cream cones for us all. There were smiles all around. It encouraged me so much that I felt like I would be able to make it through the night after all, and that my dad was only a phone call away.

Through all of my adventures in babysitting, I had a very nice savings account. I would loan out money to many members of my family. They would always pay me back, but it was pretty cool to have enough money, as a kid, to help out adults and my older siblings. My saving habits were intuitive. My parents never really talked to me about saving money or encouraged me to open a savings account. Talking to your children about money is a great idea. Just like anything else, educating your children about money will make them smarter and wiser financially. Saving is important at any age and needs to be constant. Unfortunately this habit did not follow me into adulthood.

Unlike most books or financial advice, my focus will be about saving money. There is a method to my madness based on experience. I kept reading and studying and reading more and all the authors had great, sound advice, but I was missing a huge component of the authors' plans. Many advised the number one action was to set aside money for an emergency plan, which is a super idea and wonderful move if you are able to do so.

However, I did not have any money to work with to create that emergency fund. Next step experts, like Dave

Ramsey, advise you to get rid of your debt by the snowball effect. Again grand thought, but I had that persistent problem that made that impossible—no extra money.

Saving money from what you presently spend in your everyday life is really what a lot of folks, including myself, need to do. That's why much of my book is devoted to ways to cut expenses in the weekly cash going out of your house. If you are able to cut what you are spending, then you will be able to start saving the initial $1,000 needed for the start of financial survival. Unfortunately, I was unable to save any money for quite a few years until I really sought out serious way to cut my budget.

Granted I had children graduating from eighth grade and high school, some years two children just weeks apart. Life was busy and crazy! It seemed like life was changing rapidly and required more of me, and so I was spending more money. Every time I turned around there would be a big event, or one of the kids would need equipment or school supplies. Without a doubt I had to find a way out! I can't emphasize enough how saving money on life's expenses is the first step to enable you to start the march toward financial independence. Without freeing up money, there isn't any extra to save.

In my mind my dilemma kept circling round and round that I needed a startup emergency fund and yes the authors I read were right. My bills were just too high and I didn't have any left over to save. Nonetheless, I am not a quitter and I knew there was a way out. With God's help, determination, and more wisdom I could do it. One by one I started applying all the money saving ideas included in this book, some of which took some getting used to by my family. For instance, my grocery budget is what it is. We never go without, but I try very hard to keep on track with what I have allotted for food. And so there was no money for extras, which upset some of them. Sometimes I would be a bit discouraged because it takes time for those pennies to mount up in the bank. Please don't be dismayed but persevere. It will work!

As I applied the money saving tips, my budget began to change. For a time I tried to be a coupon guru. I thought I was saving money hand over fist, but I was really just spending more. You see, I live in an area where stores do not double coupons and there is only one store that has rewards. Keeping that in mind, my couponing actually cost me more money. I finally stopped clipping coupons and buying three newspapers to do so.

My eye opener was when I started making my own laundry detergent. That saved a huge amount. After that, I started making all my own cleaners, and the savings just started piling up. With each strategy I was saving more and more money. From then on I searched, and still do, for more and more ways to save money.

In this book I only list my top ten ways to save money, but there are tons of ways I didn't mention. Choosing ten was intentional; this way you have a good solid foundation to build from. Do not stop at the ten. Keeping researching and keep learning. It will only benefit you and your family. Search the internet for ways to save more money, how to be financially independent, how to save money in the current year, and the best money saving tips are great searches to begin with. This is, at minimal, a weekly occurrence for me if not an every other day happening. Just don't get overwhelmed. Try each tip one by one, and at a good rate apply them to your household.

As I mentioned before, when you start saving money, it can easily be absorbed unless you make your savings automatic. This took me a bit to learn. I started saving a lot of money, but I quickly let it go out the window. I would save money and then just go to the movies or out to eat with it. You need to say to yourself I saved $75 this month, so I will begin having that automatically put in a savings account. As you begin to save more, you need to increase the amount that is being put in your savings account. It is astounding how quickly it will add up, which brings me to a very important point—this savings account needs to be left for emergencies until you have reached a minimum amount of three to six months of your income. If you are the sole income provider for your family, it is safer to accumulate six to twelve months of your income.

When I first realized how much I needed to save for an emergency fund, I thought it would take me forever. I want to encourage you to keep on track and keep trying because it doesn't take as long as you think it will. During the process, unforeseen problems may arise and you will experience a small setback. That is to be expected; just keep going. Life happens in every family and we experience times of great joy and moments of enormous trials. It's the resolve to keep going forward that will make the difference.

10

Clever Cleaning

I am not sure how your afternoons unwound after school as a teenager, but mine were chock full of cleaning chores at home or work at McDonald's. Before I headed anywhere for the evening, I needed to make sure the laundry was done and the house was clean. I lived with my dad and my stepmother. My dad was a very hard worker and worked two jobs, but I still needed to pick up the slack.

I have always been a very neat, tidy person. Having a clean house with four kids was doable but having a tidy house was a bit different. Making sure the deep cleaning was done like having gleaming white toilet bowls and a freshly mopped kitchen floor was imperative for me. But walking into my house and seeing toys around my house and the marks of four little ones didn't bother me.

I have tried everything I found online, in books, on television, and even the scuttlebutt of the town on how to save money, but one of the ways I slashed my expenses the most was making my own cleaning supplies. For quite some time, I was a huge advocate for clipping coupons and I thought I was such an animal, saving money left and right on cleaning supplies when I actually was spending my hard earned money on unnecessary things.

I kept coming across the suggestion of making your own laundry detergent so that's where I started. Shortly after that success, I said to myself if I can make my own detergent why can't I make my own glass cleaner, furniture polish, wood floor cleaner, and bathroom cleaner. Most cleaners have similar ingredients! The homemade ones work great and save so much money. There is a small cost to getting the main ingredients, but after that, the money saved starts adding up. Here are some of the recipes I use:

Laundry Detergent
1 box of Borax
1 cup Super Washing Soda by Arm and Hammer
1 cup of shaved soap (I use Dial because it is the cheapest)
1 hand held cheese grater to shave the soap
Container to hold the detergent
1 Tablespoon baking soda

First, I grate the bar of soap with the grater. Then I put the rest of the ingredients in a bowl and begin to mix it by hand. Then I add the soap and continue stirring until it looks thoroughly mixed. I make large amounts so I do not have to do it so frequently.

Furniture Polish

1 Tablespoon of olive oil
¾ of a cup of water
4 Tablespoons of vinegar
30 drops of lemon juice
1 spray bottle
4 drops of essential oil (for fragrance)

I put this in an old spray bottle and spray it on my furniture. It makes it easy to use.

Glass Cleaner

2 spray bottles
½ cup of rubbing alcohol
½ cup of vinegar
½ liter of water
1 Tablespoon of lemon juice
4 Tablespoons of dish detergent
3 drops of blue food coloring (optional)

Again I put this in an old glass cleaner bottle so I am able to use it easily.

Wood Floor Cleaner

1 squirt bottle from a wood floor cleaning product
3 Tablespoons of vinegar
16 ounces of warm water
3 drops of essential oil
1 teaspoon of olive oil

I put this in an old wood floor cleaner bottle. This way I can evenly squirt it on my wood floors. It works like a charm.

Bathroom Cleaner
3 Tablespoons of baking soda
3 Tablespoons of Vinegar
3 drops of essential oil
One Spray Bottle

Fill the remainder of the bottle with water.

Dish Washing Detergent
1 Tablespoon Borax
1 Tablespoon super washing soda
1 teaspoon of baking soda
1 Tablespoon of vinegar
3 Tablespoons of lemon juice

Please take note: this particular concoction will act a little like a tiny volcano. I purposely mix this over the dishwasher (not the sink) so when it reacts and flows over the bowl, it hits the spot.

It will take a little bit of time and effort, but if you follow these tips, you will see such savings that it will shock you. Detergent and cleaners are very expensive and in my opinion way overpriced!

11

Outdoor Oasis

The outdoors is an awesome playground to save lots of money. The second year of owning our home, we decided to plant three apple trees. It really was my husband's idea. I had never gardened and certainly we didn't have apple trees growing up. Wade and I drove to the local greenhouse and picked out the apple trees. I thought, *Okay, now we just throw those puppies in the ground or what?* I had no clue of what the next step should be. Note there is a lot of hope for you city slickers that haven't had much of a green thumb. That used to be me. My parents nor anyone in the family gardened very much. Oh we did have some flowers here and there but never any fruits or vegetables. Gardening was foreign to me.

Wade and I strolled out to the country greenhouse and picked out three beautiful apple trees and headed home. We put on our gloves, grabbed a shovel, and headed to the back-yard to find the perfect spots for each one. Since I didn't know the first thing about gardening, I was anxious to see how this unfolded.

Wade seemed to know a bit more than I did but was still a novice. We dug, toiled, and eventually planted the trees. I thought to myself, *Let's see what will happen now.* To my pleasant surprise the trees grew well and continue to provide wintertime crispy apple years later. Planting fruit trees and fruit bushes are excellent sources of free groceries. Every year I freeze at least 12 to 16 bags of apples to last for the winter. I freeze my raspberries as well. Gardening does take time, effort, good soil, sun, and God's touch but is deliciously worth it.

Yearly Garden

Along with fruit trees, a yearly garden is a must. Since I work two jobs, I am very busy, but my yearly garden is a savings I can't afford to miss. Depending on the growing season that year, different vegetables will produce a better crop. None of us can predict the growing season, but knowing your climate and area is very helpful. For example, I live in northern Maine where onions, green beans, cucumbers, squash, pumpkins, and most of the time corn are dependable crops. Those are my staples. Some years tomatoes may do well and other year's green peppers may excel. The point is that you need to know what are reliable crops for your area.

With my commodities from the garden I able to freeze, can, and cook delectable food. It just wouldn't be right if I didn't explain at least one example of each. Let's take pumpkins first. I plant them early in the year because they need at least 90 days or more to grow. Once they are ready to be harvested, I mosey on down to my garden and put my "green thumb" (ha-ha) into action.

Freezing Pumpkin

The first step is one of the hardest. Take a sharp knife and quarter the pumpkin. Then grab a strong spoon or ice cream scoop to gut the pumpkin's seeds and stringy insides out. Place the pumpkin on a cookie sheet and bake at 375 degrees for at least one hour. Remove the pumpkin from the oven. Use a pot holder and take one quartered pumpkin piece and begin to spoon the cooked pumpkin into a bowl, leaving the skin to be discarded. Once you have done this with all four quarters of the pumpkin, take a hand masher and mash the pumpkin up. If it is extra juicy, you may want to put it in a strainer for a minute or two. Measure one or two cups of pumpkin and use a vacuum sealer to seal the desired amount. Now just place in the freezer until you need it.

Canning Tomatoes

Okay, where do I begin with this one? Out of the three items I am sharing about, this one has quite a few steps, but it allows the tomatoes to last for a long time. For starters it is best to flash steam tomatoes in order to easily skin them. This entails washing the tomatoes and cutting a small x at the top. Next bring a pot of water to a boil. While that is heating, get a bowl of ice ready. Once the water is boiling, put the tomatoes in it for about 30 seconds or until you see the skin loosening. Remove them immediately and place in the ice bowl. Then carefully peel the entire skin off.

Now you are ready to start cooking them and eventually canning them. Cut up seven tomatoes and cook them for 40 minutes on the stove. Prepare your canning jars as you would for any canning project. Fill the jars about ¾ full of cooked tomatoes. Add 2 tablespoons of lemon juice and ¼ of an inch of tomato juice. The last step is to cook for 10 minutes in a pressure cooker. I know it seems like a lengthy process, but remember it's all natural; no chemicals were added, and they will last for quite some time.

Storing Onions for the Winter

Onions grow well up our way and last me most of the winter. Some clues that let you know when they are ready to be harvested are: when you see the onion tops fall over and lean sideways toward the ground, or when the bulbs look fairly large and mature. Then they may be pulled up. Once you have picked them, they need to be placed in a shaded temperate room to cure.

After a few days you cut the tops off and let them sit for a few more days, at least three. At this point you will need an oversized mesh laundry bag. It needs to have holes in it so air is getting to the onions or they will rot when storing them. I place them hanging up in my basement for the fall and winter. Wouldn't you know it, Miss Advice here had to watch a video to clarify these instructions. To my family and me, they taste so much better than store bought onions.

Try one thing at a time and take it slow. The internet has a plethora of information to help guide you through it. Like anything new, the more you do it, the easier it becomes.

12

Creative Cooking

Years ago looking at my two beautiful babies in my freezing, lousy apartment, I thought to myself that I needed to do something to help provide for these sweet blessings. One important craft I could do was to learn to cook from scratch so I could save on groceries. Remember, my husband and I were determined to take care of our children without government assistance. I thought if I could tackle the art of cooking and baking the basics, oh boy, the money I would save.

One of my first adventures I decided to embark on was making homemade frosting. I absolutely love home baked goodies, so I felt it would be a perk knowing how to make frosting. At the time, I didn't own a computer so trial and error was my plan of action. Unfortunately it seemed to go more on the side of error rather than trial.

Anyone who has or has had two small babies at the same time understands cooking can be a chore, period, let alone if you don't know what you're doing. But I gathered all the ingredients and began making mistakes. They came one right after another. I had my sister-in-law's scrumptious chocolate frosting recipe. I followed every step with great precision, or so I thought. Here it was the end of the mixing and the beginning of noticing what an epic fail my first try was. I tried to spread the liquid gel on a sweet, white cake.

With every swipe I thought, *What is the matter with this frosting?* It bothered me all night long. *What did I do wrong?* I even asked God to help me understand why the frosting was as thin as water. I needed some divine help, you know what I am saying. Finally it dawned on me, I had put in 1¼ cups of milk instead of only ¼ cup of milk.

My first journeys in the kitchen gave me a great realization—I wasn't naturally the greatest chef. Well, honestly, I wasn't even a good prep cook. I had a lot to learn and tons of mistakes to make. If you're not a whiz in the kitchen, do not worry. Don't think for one minute every one of those professional chefs and bakers you have seen on television and in magazines haven't made tons of mistakes in their career because they have. The truth is, we learn by messing up. As you read this book you might say to yourself that you don't even cook let alone bake. You are more than capable of teaching yourself to do both. Trust me I wasn't good at it either, but I had a huge passion—I love to eat!

It is now time to reveal one of my favorite money savings tips of all: cook everything you can at home, I mean everything you are able to. Having basic ingredients to cook and bake with are necessary. For baking you need to have flour, brown sugar, confectionary sugar, white sugar, peanut butter, spices, shortening, chocolate baking chips, baking powder and soda, eggs, butter, and different types of extract. You're thinking that's quite a list, and yes it is, but think of what you can create with it and the money you will save; it's a good move.

I have to say I now truly enjoy baking and delight in eating it. I have quite a sweet tooth. One of my favorite recipes is peanut butter balls. Here is a recipe, but I will admit when it comes to baking I do not measure a thing—only the first time I try the recipe and then I cook or bake it to my taste.

Peanut Butter Balls

Center of the peanut butter ball:
1 cup of peanut butter
2 Tablespoons of butter
½ cup of brown sugar
½ cup of confectionary sugar

Mix the above ingredients together.

Top and bottom layers:
2 bags of semi-sweet chocolate baking chips
2 tablespoons of shortening

Carefully melt the chips and shortening in the microwave, stirring frequently until it is smooth.

Fill mini muffin liners halfway with the chocolate. Roll the peanut butter center into a small ball and place it on top of the chocolate. Lastly pour more chocolate on top. Once they are cool, they are mouthwatering. I make them ahead of time, wrap them in plastic, and freeze them for the holidays.

Cooking meals include using some of the same ingredients along with many other different ones. Our family's taste is more like hometown cooking. So I always have potatoes, meat, veggies, loads of spices, lots of condiments, and many different types of dressings on hand. This will vary with your family's taste. Be sure to have readily available supplies to match the cooking you desire. An easy recipe I like that isn't too time consuming is Chicken Divan.

Chicken Divan

About 2 pounds of boneless chicken breast
1 can of cheddar cheese soup
1 package frozen broccoli
3 cups of shredded cheese

Cut the chicken breast up into small pieces about the length of a green bean, fry it in a little oil, and season to your taste with salt and pepper. Microwave the broccoli for a few minutes or steam it, but make sure to remove it before it is completely cooked. Take an 8½ inch by 11 inch pan and spread the chicken and broccoli in it. In a separate dish pour in the soup and mix it with ¾ cup of milk. Now add the chicken and broccoli. While you're mixing, sprinkle one cup of the cheddar cheese in it. Save the other two cups and pour over the top after you have it thoroughly mixed. Bake at 350 degrees for 40 minutes.

Along with cooking most of your food at home, making a double batch is like making a deposit in the bank. Recently I have started cooking or preparing double batches of supper. We will eat one for that night and freeze the other for a night when I am stuck at work, the kids have me involved in some activity, or I just do not have the time or inclination to cook. As many families are, we are constantly busy and on the go. All moms out there understand those crazy nights when cooking supper is nearly impossible, but it costs a lot of money to get take out for a family of six. For about a year, I have been making double batches, and it has relieved those stressful nights. It also alleviates the pressure the family puts on Mom or Dad to have dinner ready regardless of the night's events.

One of the easiest recipes to make is chili. You are welcome to use a variety of ingredients within this recipe either with the beans or chili mix.

Chili

2 pounds hamburger meat
2 packages of chili mix
2 cans of pinto beans drained (or any of your choice)
A large jar of salsa or two smaller ones
Shredded cheddar cheese

Fry the hamburger in a pan. Drain the grease and add one package of chili mix with the water needed. Put it in a crock pot. Add a jar of salsa and the drained beans to the hamburger. Cook on low five to six hours. Add desired cheese when you serve it. Now do the same with the other half except do not put it in a crock pot but rather in a container you can store in the freezer. And that's a wrap for two supper dishes.

These are but a few recipes you can try. There are lots of great ones you can look up on the internet that are easy and will match your family's tastes. Some sites even let you accumulate the recipes you are interested in by created a virtual recipe box so you can easily find the one you need.

13

Negotiate Naggers

Anyone do well in debate class? If you answered yes, this chapter is definitely for you. We can all think of the time we decided to speak up and say our piece. Some of those times we were hailed as heroes and other times we were noted as the one who shoved his or her foot in her mouth.

This very thought takes me back to the Bible when Moses decided to remind God of His mercy and beg for God not to destroy His creation. If Moses wasn't bold enough to try to change God's mind, how would the history of man be different today? What would the result have been? (See Numbers 14:11-19.) Many of the great people who shaped this world were ones who were willing to speak up. Now I realize I am not asking us all to write to our local legislators to change laws, but there are times when you will need to speak up on your family's behalf.

Here's the thing we need to remember—all the companies and businesses we deal with want our money. Knowing this we have the upper hand. No cable company or cell phone provider wants to lose you as a customer. Play that hand and play it well. The more faithful you have been in making payments, the more cards you hold. This money saving tip will take a little negotiating on your behalf. First go through your current bills like your cell phone, insurance, and cable. Look for extra expenses for services you really do not use and do not care if you have. One of the first bills I changed was my television plan. I chose a different plan and that lowered my bill a bit. My next move included calling the provider directly and stating that unless it was cheaper, I would be cancelling my subscription. Please keep in mind when doing this, it is important to use good manners and be polite but firm. The company willingly gave me discounts without any hassles.

Even with these changes we were still paying about $84 a month. I needed to up the ante. At this point I had haggled with the provider as much as they would allow. So I decided to switch providers, which granted me a higher savings for two years. When that savings expired, I called the provider and explained that unless my bill was discounted, I would switch back. At that time my current provider gave me ten more months of discounts. (If it weren't for my family, I would ditch the satellite and watch online or get some monthly movie package like Netflix.)

I like my current provider especially because they offer local news. I guess you would call it local, although it comes from about an hour away. Again it reverts to the problem of being in a one horse town. Most of the satellite signals come out of larger cities and some are not near us. So if I am with other providers, I may end up with local news coming from New York. Small things like this may have an impact on your decision.

With six of us under our auto insurance plan, the monthly bill was about $330. That is quite a hefty bill to keep us just driving vehicles. I needed to slash that bill somehow. Well, my car is a 2008 model, has 110,000 miles on it, and has been paid off for quite a while, so there really wasn't a need to have all the extra insurance I had on it. My son's car was similar. To save money I switched to liability only on those two vehicles. You will only be able to do this if your car is paid for. I would only recommend this if two components are present—it has quite a few miles on it and is completely paid for. Cha ching! More money saved.

Last but not least look at an itemized bill for your cell phone(s). Do you need all the data you are paying for? Do you have an extra line as a home line? Would a different plan be cheaper? Again we have six cell phones in our house so my bill became more like a car payment. I dropped a line I used as a home line and then changed my plan a bit, and it has saved more money. Make sure to do your research first because if you lessen your data and happen to go over, you'll be paying more than before. Any one of these three suggestions puts money in the bank.

Another perk to watch for is the new customer gimmicks. One evening I was watching television and saw a commercial from my cell phone provider offering new customers more data for a cheaper price than I was paying. Minutes later I was on my phone negotiating. When the call was finished, my family had more data for a better price. Keep in mind you get more bees with honey so approach these companies pleasantly and not in a defensive manner. Usually they are more than willing to accommodate to keep you as a customer.

14

Shop Smart

Using our head can be a super saver. This next chapter takes a bit of time, but anything that frees up money is worth the investment of our time. Let's first take a journey into the Old Testament to see some wisdom in action.

The scenario plays out in 1 Kings 3:16-28. Two women approach Solomon, king of Israel, in a horrible predicament. One of the women's babies had died during the night and one was still alive. Each woman was claiming that the child still living was theirs. Solomon was asked to judge them. Keep in mind that God blessed Solomon with wisdom beyond his years.

Hearing each one of these women's account of the night gave no direction to the king. He decided to propose an inhumane idea of taking the living baby and cutting it in half; giving each mother one half. He knew the love of the true mother would forbid such a thought. She immediately spoke up and begged the king not to go forward. At this point, Solomon knew she was the true mother and gave her the living child. Wisdom is priceless when put into practice.

On a weekly basis I scour the local store circulars to see

what is on sale. Remember I live in a smaller town so there are not tons of stores to choose from, but we do have three grocery stores. I have a weekly budget for groceries and I stick to it for the most part. It's important you set that limit for yourself.

Taking the three weekly ads, I begin to look closely for the food my family enjoys. During the week when you run out of essentials, write them down so you remember to buy those first. I have my phone handy to create the list. On my list I write the items and where they are found, keeping in mind how much money I have to spend. After you do this for a while, you become familiar with how far your money will stretch.

In a smaller town like the one I live in, you really need to hit the store the day of the sale or you may be waiting until a mid-week shipment comes to get the item or wind up getting a rain check. The longer you do this, the better you become with knowing what a good deal is and the time of year to stock up on certain items. For example, the spaghetti sauce our family likes goes on sale in the early fall so I stock up for the year.

Before hitting the local stores for your weekly shopping trip, check your list for what you need, what's on sale and where, and how much money you have to work with, so you plan your trip carefully and don't exceed your weekly budget. The longer you do this, the more you will have stored in your cabinets.

You can stock up on items that last a long time at a cheaper price and save them for a later date. Also some stores have what they call BOGOs—buy one and get one free. That's an easy way of spending the same amount for an item but having another one in reserve. Mayonnaise is a good one for that strategy as it is frequently one of the BOGO items and is so cost effective that way. Research the stores in your area to find which ones have deals like this and plan accordingly.

Speaking of dates, to lengthen the shelf life of my groceries I always reach for the back jar with the later expiration date. Being a smart shopper saves the dough.

Grocery shopping can be a large expense but there are many great strategies for saving money there.

15

Crafty Cash

When I was 16 years old, I remember my father emphatically stating that I was to come home with a job or not to come home at all. Now you have to understand that my dad was a loving man who meant very well. He just felt like I had too much time on my hands and needed to get myself moving.

I looked around my hometown, Stafford, Connecticut, and like most teenagers in the U.S.A., I knew I could head to McDonald's. So that afternoon I borrowed my dad's car and drove right down there. I asked to speak with a manager and began a face-to-face interview that they didn't even know was coming. I knew I couldn't return home without some type of job. After my unexpected interview, I had a job.

A job is a way to bring income your way. In my case now I work one full-time job and a second part-time job. Both have been a tremendous help, and I feel very fortunate to have them because they are one way to bring money in your direction. So this next portion of the book is dedicated to scraping up some extra coins.

An impressive but surprising way to make money is to sell some of your stuff. When I implemented this avenue of making money, I was shocked at the money I made in our small little town. In the fall I go through our entire house, weeding out unused items and cleaning every nook and cranny. Usually I give all my collected items away. As of recently, I started doing a yearly yard/garage sale. After the sale is over, I give all of the unsold items to the local Project Graduation.

When doing a yard sale, the following are some helpful hints. First, make sure you advertise in the local paper and post a very large sign in your front yard, which is a huge key to success. Without a good marketing plan, no one will know the sale is going on. Always have all your items marked with a price. When pricing your items, keep in mind negotiating with your customers. Have different amounts of change so you don't have to turn a potential customer away if they only have a larger bill.

One huge piece of advice is to know what your items are worth. It is very important to do your homework here. Now granted, you may not get what the item is valued at, but you will have a ball park figure to work with. Boy, did I get burned in this area. At one of my sales I sold a very valuable item because I had no idea it was worth so much. The item was never returned to me. I was just told how badly I was ripped off.

Another thought is incorporating your crafty talents in the sale. I am not the crafty type, but baking is right up my alley. For weeks before the sale, I bake tons of goodies and freeze them. That way I can take them out as needed. I also advertise that I am selling homemade baked goods. The following recipe is one of my best sellers. Maine is famous for whoopie pies. I had never heard of a whoopie pie before moving to northern Maine, but oh, are they absolutely delectable!

Pumpkin Chocolate Chip Whoopie Pies

3 cups of flour
2 cups of brown sugar
1½ cans of pumpkin
2 eggs
2 tablespoons of milk
1 cup of oil
1 teaspoon vanilla
1 teaspoon cinnamon
1 teaspoon ginger
1 teaspoon baking powder
1 teaspoon baking powder
24 ounces of chocolate chips

First combine all the liquid ingredients. Once you have mixed them slowly, add the dry ingredients. Mix the chocolate chips in by hand. Using an ice cream scoop to measure, place six full scoops on a cooking sheet. Bake at 350 degrees for 12-15 minutes. As they are baking, start the frosting (recipe below).

Frosting

4 cups of confectionary sugar
½ cup of butter (1 stick)
½ cup of shortening
2 tablespoons of milk

Make sure the butter is soft before mixing with the buttermilk and shortening. Add the sugar in slowly until the frosting is creamy.

Let the pumpkin chocolate chip whoopie pie cool. Then take one whoopie pie and lather frosting on. Top it off with another whoopie pie. I wrap in saran wrap and freeze to have on hand when needed, especially around the holidays.

Ebay was another street I traveled down. In my cellar, my cabinets, and the garage, I had loads and loads of old collectable items. Many of them were my grandmother's and did she ever have an eye for value. The yard sale got me started in good shape, but some of the most valuable items I was selling were still left on the tables. A majority of the remaining items I gave to charity, but I hung onto my gram's antiques and collectable items

I had sold some of my items to the local antique shops but of course they didn't want to pay very much and certainly not what they were worth. A couple of the guys I was dealing with told me not to sell my stuff on eBay because it charges too many fees. Well I thought to myself I never mentioned eBay, it must be worth trying. So I did.

Setting up an account wasn't very hard at all. Their website leads you through the process easily. Along with setting up an eBay account, you will need to set up a PayPal account. One warning I would give to you is that PayPal does not need your social security number. Once you have both of those up and running, with strong passwords assigned to both, it's time to get off the ground. You can use your smart phone to take the pictures of the items you are selling. My iPhone has a very thick protective case so it doesn't take great pictures. I use my camera to take very appealing pictures with a good background. Then I download the pictures to my computer and then upload them on eBay.

Some of the mistakes I've made selling items on eBay were costly and very avoidable. It's quite exciting at first to see people viewing your items, bidding on them, and finally purchasing them. I was extremely enthusiastic about selling items so I would compromise on my shipping cost, especially if someone bought two items from me. It is fine to do combined shipping, but do not underestimate how much it will cost you. I sure did a couple of times and it cost me quite a bit.

Mistake number two was not posting enough specifics about the items. The more information you have posted, the more interest you will create. Measure your item with accuracy, list any specifics, and always tell your buyers to feel free to ask any questions.

Don't get discouraged if you don't sell your item. When I first got started, I thought if it didn't sell after it was relisted three times, I'd better take it off and discount it. I was completely wrong. Now I keep about 50 items on eBay for sale and keep relisting them. I make sure I am able to relist for free. I have found that eventually your item does sell. There always is someone out there who will love what you are selling. But do not try selling junk at a high price because that won't work well. What I usually do is research what I am selling and do a price comparison so my prices are fair and competitive.

Here are two positive ways to boost your selling power. One is to be an effective communicator. When my item sells, I send an itemized bill and then write a note at the bottom thanking them. Once the buyer has paid for the item, I contact them immediately to thank them, letting them know when I am planning on mailing the item and posting the tracking number. After I have mailed the item, I again post the tracking number and let them know I did. The more customer service your provide, the better your ranking on eBay, which causes potential customers to view you as a safe vendor.

Making sure you are quick to mail a purchased item is also a must. Buyers want their items as soon as possible. Life is busy and I understand that, but it is good practice to get the items mailed fast. Making sure they are packed well is just as important. All the items I sell are put in bubble wrap and placed in secure bubble wrapped envelopes or boxes. An easy way is to order bubble wrap padded envelopes from the USPS. For more positive PR I also send a small thank you note with the item.

Using eBay is an easy way to sell your unwanted possessions. Be aware, however, eBay does charge you 10% and PayPal charges you a small fee too. It is still better than getting nothing for stuff you don't even want. You know the old saying, "One person's trash is another's treasure." Give it a shot. It's not too hard to get started, and it only takes a little maintenance to keep it going. I try to check my eBay account each day and once I sell three or four items, I replace them with another three or four. It hasn't made me rich, but it has helped unload some unwanted items and put more cash in my hand. Remember every little bit helps.

How badly do you want to be financially stable or out of debt? Do have the work ethic and determination to make it happen? It may be a long road, but when you reach the destination the journey doesn't seem that bad. It is a true juggling act to work two jobs, take care of the children, and keep the house up, not to mention, the other community responsibilities you may have. Trust me I completely understand.

For quite a few years I have been working with the youth at my church, which is one more activity that takes up time and effort. I feel very blessed to have had such an opportunity but again it is another night to prepare for and be out of the house. Each one of us has reasons we are too busy and why it would be difficult to work a second job. I know I sure did, but I also knew I needed to do something or we would be in trouble.

Where I live is an economically challenged area. Wages are not very high, and it costs a lot more to live way up here in the north. For the past six years I have worked a second job. My main job is teaching second grade, but I also waitress at a local restaurant. During the summer I teach summer school part-time and work full-time at the restaurant. During the fall and winter, I am at school full-time and still work at the restaurant two nights a week.

Working during the summer helps me save money to take my family on vacation, pay for back-to-school supplies for my children, and buy more groceries to stock up for the winter.

During the winter my second job helps pay for my weekly gas and aids in buying groceries. You need to be diligent if you live where it take a little more to squeak by.

Busy is part of many people's vocabulary, and I am one of them. Working a second job puts a capitol B in Busy. There are many mornings when I wake up and think, *Oh my, here we go, a 15 to 17 hour day coming my way!* Now some of those double shifts are only 13 hour days. Those double shift days I bring my uniform for the restaurant to school, do an outfit change after school, and zoom off to the next round.

Any of you who have waitressed also realize some of those long days are not as profitable as others. For example, living in a small community such as this sales plummet when winters are very long. But I thank God for any money I do make. As I have mentioned before, any small step can be a great help. Working my second job has made me realize, more than any other thing I have done, how every dollar adds up.

Some days it seems hard having to work so many hours, but then I think how fortunate I am to be able to hold two jobs with the health and ability to work them. I am always trying to find a higher paying job, with at least the same benefits, and one that interests me. Teaching children is a passion of mine, but truthfully I do not want to work two jobs the rest of my life.

Maine is one of the lowest paying states for teachers. Of course that's the career I chose. For the past ten years, I have been teaching and have thoroughly enjoyed it. I will continue my two jobs until either I find a better one or have financially stabilized our household so my teaching job is enough. Until one option is reached, I will keep my hands on the shovel and continue to gain financial ground for my family.

Gas prices can be obnoxious. We can spend so much money on traveling back and forth, but if we planned a little better, we could save lots of money in that area too. With this in mind, I understand multiple trips are inevitable with children involved with extracurricular activities. There are those infamous nights where you have to drag the family here and there to attend multiple events. Those nights are too complicated to apply this method.

On a routine week, plan out your grocery and banking trips. My husband is notorious for going into town three times on Saturday. I will say to him, "Why don't you go to the bank when you are going to the dump?" Later in the day he will head out the third time to go to the store. I just shake my head and wish he understood the money he is wasting.

Throughout the week pre-plan your trips to the business district of your town. This takes a little thinking ahead, but it will help you out. If you need to bank on Fridays, think about what else you can do the same day to avoid having to travel back on a different day. If you have an appointment in town, try to plan your weekly shopping trip for that day. I always did my grocery shopping while my youngest daughter was at dance class. You end up killing two birds with one stone. Anything that saves money makes sense.

Another aspect of saving money while traveling is carpooling to work or school. If you have a neighbor or someone in close proximity that works at the same place, perhaps you could share the ride. It would cut your gas bill in half instantly. On top of slashing the gas bill, it gives you company for the ride to work. One of my children attends college at the University of Maine in Presque Isle but still lives with us. Each week she takes turns with a friend traveling up to Presque Isle to save money. She only has one class she had to attend there, but it is in session twice a week. This way they both save money and aren't taking an hour long ride by themselves. Carpooling definitely has both financial and social benefits.

Throughout my research I found multiple examples of people who walk or bike to work. In this neck of the woods, it is a near impossible feat. Our temperatures are too bitter and dangerous to do in the winter. Another road bump in that idea way up here is that we are a very rural community. Most of the residents live at least ten miles from their current occupation. However, if you live in an urban area, it could save you oodles.

This next money saver idea I have been using the longest—saving money on your electric bill. Every saving point has a small initial investment. To begin with, I changed the light bulbs in my house to efficiency light bulbs. As I kept trying to lessen our electricity usage, I started unplugging appliances. I do caution you if your children use your appliances, be careful with large appliances like your dyer. I stopped unplugging my dryer when one of my middle children said she got a small shock plugging it in one day (side note she was 19 years old). However, I still keep my toaster, coffee pot, and microwave unplugged unless I am using them.

For my television, I got a power strip and a surge protector so when the television is off so is the power strip. This has helped save a tremendous amount. I did the same with my computer and printer. When they are not in use, you can just switch them off. It conserves quite a bit of energy. This was one of my family's most challenging and frustrating adjustment to make. Now when we turn on the television we have to wait for the satellite to load, which only takes about two minutes. The whining and complaining I heard when I first implemented this idea was ridiculous. Thankfully the complaints have stopped and they have accepted this maneuver.

This next piece of advice is just plain common sense—turn off the lights you are not using especially if you leave the room. We all leave lights on that are not being used. Just remember to pay attention to what lights you have on.

My husband is a carpenter so we have been able to insulate our house well and check for energy leaks. We have added a lot of insulation in our attic and on our house when we put siding on it. Replacing your windows also tightens leaks. It is worth it to have an energy audit by a professional to see where you are wasting energy. Every small bit of change adds up.

16

Do the DIY

Remember the first push of those pedals with those training wheels off? We practiced over and over again. Up and down the road we pedaled with those training wheels on, preparing for the day they would be removed. Then we felt ready. It was the day, the time, and the very minute to try it. Dad would ask if we were ready and our response would be, "Yeah," answered with anticipation and hesitation all at the same time. We pushed one foot down and began to pedal. We may have been a bit wobbly at first but we keep striving harder. We all may have fallen a time or two or maybe three or four, but how proud were we. We did it! We could hardly believe it. No longer did we need those training wheels. We were free!

Taking on more responsibility, just like riding without training wheels, helps us to strive harder, dig deeper, and care more. The more effort we put forth, the more accomplished we feel when the job is done. Many points in this book have a reference to the term DIY: Do it yourself. If we pour the foundation, frame in the house, and stud up the walls, decorating is the icing on the cake. The more we can do ourselves, the more money we save and the more gratification we have in what has been done.

Wedding Planning

My oldest daughter is getting married shortly. When she began dating the man she is marrying, she kept dropping hints my way about how soon there would be a proposal and then marriage. When I finally caught on to it, I suggested she and I open a wedding fund account. So that's exactly what we did. Both of us began contributing a monthly amount into the account. It was surprising how rapidly it added up. (On the other hand, it was as equally shocking how quickly they got engaged and planned a wedding date.)

Being a step ahead is much better than having to charge your way through an event. Now do understand, at this point we have already blown through the wedding stash and are buying items monthly to keep up. Within the plans we have saved a lot of money by the famous DIY attitude. We have planned the meal—lasagna, salad, rolls, and cake. I will be making lasagnas shortly and freezing them. Many of the drinks and other needed items for the wedding I have purchased through stores like Sam's Club where I can buy in bulk and save money. We opted to make the bouquets with fake flowers ourselves. Watching You Tube "how to" videos are stupendous ways to accomplish unfamiliar tasks. We saved a bundle by this step.

The bridal shower will be hosted at my house and catered by the maid of honor and myself. Again more work but again more money saved. I have baked all kinds of delicious desserts and frozen them so we will have tons to munch on. The cupcakes I will make fresh the day before. All the other food I will incorporate in my weekly grocery shopping. Prizes for the games I picked up here and there on clearance.

We devoted many nights to comparing prices for decorations online. We purchased what we could each month so there was never an enormous amount of money spent at any one time. The DIY way does put more work and pressure upon you, but the dollars sure do add up. By no means are we pulling off a royal wedding, but it will be very quaint and stylish.

With all the resources out there, a wedding planner isn't necessary for a smaller wedding like ours. There are wonderful websites that tell you exactly what you need to accomplish and by what month it needs to be done. These particular helps have made planning a wedding much easier. Keep in mind I work two jobs, so time is very important is my schedule. Referring back to these lists and bouncing thoughts continually off one another has gotten us this far and hopefully will bring us through a beautiful wedding without charging thousands. With some heavy duty planning, teaming up, and working through the glitches, you too can be the wedding planner.

Creating a wedding with a budget could be a book in itself. These were just a few suggestions that helped me though my daughter's wedding. There are books, magazines, websites, and friends who have already been there to consult to keep the ball rolling. Using as many resources as you can is the key. Call in those favors and lean on those friends. Weddings are plenty of work and you need help to pull them off. Don't be shy in asking for assistance from others.

Do the DIY

Remodeling and Repairing

The new term being constantly thrown around in the re-modeling world is DIY, do it yourself. With the abundance of resources we are privy to, doing a project yourself has never been so easy. Fixing small items around the house isn't as hard as it looks. Calling a professional in costs a lot more money. Of course, in some instances it's necessary to use one. If it is a big project or problem and your spouse or you do not have the knowledge needed on the subject, I would definitely call on an expert if at all possible.

Remodeling your home yourself is an easy way to save money on labor. I am one of the messiest painters I know, but who do you think has painted most of the rooms in our house? That's right—messy me. It drives my husband crazy when he sees a paintbrush in my hand. I always try to reas-sure him that in the end it will be fine. And it is. If someone as messy as me can transform a room with a gallon of paint, so can you.

When some minuscule items aren't working, it makes a huge difference in the household running smoothly. For ex-ample, when my sink is plugged or problematic, I grab the plunger and then let Drano finish the job.

My kitchen cabinets are as old as dirt but still very func-tional. Some of the screws holding the handles are stripped so badly they fall out. I just pop a broken toothpick in with the screw and it works like a charm. Speaking about my cabi-nets, to give them a fresh look I once removed the hardware, sanded them, painted them with primer, and then plastered a fresh new color on. What a difference!

When my front load washer is flashing a warning to me, I first take off the cover and unscrew the drain to check the trap for any mysterious items. Usually that will clear up the problem; if not, it is still a good idea to clean the trap out. Don't limit what you are capable of.

Whenever you come across a problem at your house, look it up online, read a book about it, or ask a friend who has knowledge in that area. Once you have done some digging, determine if you can tackle the problem yourself. If it seems too complicated, phone for some help. It may amaze you what procedures are explained online step by step. You'll be surprised how many times you can be the answer. Happy home fixing!

Nutrition

Supply most of your daily nutritional needs from home. My teaching job allows me to bring my lunch and snacks from home very easily. My classroom holds a small microwave I purchased. This way I am able to take lunch and heat it up each work day. Having the microwave in my classroom eliminates waiting in the cafeteria line. Another step I take to ease packing my own lunch is to cook enough supper to have extra for lunch. This is a simple move but saves a bundle.

Some students do not bring snacks to school so I always have crackers or something for them and myself. If I am on top of my game during the weekend, I will cook popcorn on the stove and add butter and salt. When I pack it in zip lock baggies, it will stay fresh for the next day. It makes quite a bit and oh how tasty it is.

Do the DIY

So now I have conquered my lunch and snacks throughout the day. The only nutritional need left is fluids to last the day. I have an enormous water jug that I jam pack with ice cubes and then fill with water. Due the amount of ice cubes, my water stays nice and cold till at least 2:00 pm. If I have to work until 4:00 or later I am fine without any water for a bit. Packing my drinks for the day is a truly smart move. Think about how many dollar bills would fly out the window during the run of 8 or 9 hours.

I have to own up to drinking at least one cup of coffee a day. I bought a one cup coffee maker and brought it to my classroom as well. I brew one cup and add my delicious creamer and voila—la café de la classroom. Again I am saving myself money and making my day better.

Supplying what I need for the day has saved me a bundle. It's always comforting and nice to know you have what you need. I will admit there are some days I pack cereal and potato chips because nothing was left over from supper the night before. This lunch brings a great laugh in the teacher's room because the cereal I pick is usually one like Lucky Charms or Boo Berry. Hey, it works!

Think about how much you spend daily on lunch, multiply that times five, and then multiply that answer by forty-eight. In a nutshell that is how much you would save if you work year round, five days a week, minus four weeks for vacation time. If you crunch the numbers, you will see the savings.

17

Multiply Money

Seeing our money increase rapidly is highly motivating. The Bible has a prime example about how important it is to use the financial knowledge we have to see the results multiply. Let's set the stage. There was a man about to travel to a distant country who had various servants. He allotted goods and talents to three of them who stayed behind. When he divvied out the talents, he expected a great return.

The first servant was given five talents (money in that day). That servant used what was given to him and returned with his original five talents and gained five more. The next servant followed suit by taking his two talents and doubling them as well. Now here is where the lesson is learned. The last servant was given one talent and decided to hide his talent—not sharing it with anyone and not gaining anything.

The lord of the servants returned to see how each handled their talents and used what was given to him. We too are given special talents by God and are also blessed with people in our lives that God allows to bestow wisdom upon us. If we choose not to use what God has given us or exposed us to, we suffer and others involved in our lives do as well. Don't waste what you have been blessed with and what you have been lucky enough to be taught.

When the master spoke with the first servant, he commended him and made him ruler over much. He dealt with the next servant, in the same way complimenting him on how good and faithful the servant he was and also making him ruler over more. When he came to the servant having one talent and no increase, he delivered harsh, strong words. He removed the servant's one talent and gave it to the one that had five. Lastly he cast that servant to outer darkness (Matt. 25:15-30).

I am talking to you from a financial perspective but I also want you to think of the previous parable in a spiritual aspect as well, the way the scripture is intended to be perceived. Share what God has done for you throughout your life. Someone needs to hear it.

Certificates of Deposit

Through my weekly investigation of how to make more money, I stumbled across the idea of opening Certificate of Deposits (CDs) at the bank. Note that interest rates at banks are very low and are not yielding much at this time.

I chose to do three month renewal CDs by opening one CD in a month like July, for example, let's say for $1,000. Then I opened another CD exactly one month later for $1,000. At last I opened one more CD for $1,000 at exactly one month from the most recent one. The reason behind having three CDs one month apart is that at any time you need to take out any of the money, you will have it available to you without penalty. The idea is not to use the money but we all know sometimes life throws you unexpected curve balls. Try to just leave it and let it grow!

CDs are good ideas due to their perks. They are not as easy to access as a savings account. A savings account is just a transfer or withdrawal away, but the CDs are locked away for thirty days. If you spend money easily and have trouble holding on to it, this will help get you started. You are less tempted to take the money and hit the mall. You would have to hold onto that desire to blow your hard earned money for something for an entire thirty days, which gives you plenty of time to think about it. Impulse spending would be wiped out of the picture.

CDs also renew automatically every three months. You will not have to go to the bank or fill out more paperwork. It is set in a cycle as long as you originally arrange it that way with your bank. Yielding more than saving accounts with less accessibility is a double positive. With the current bank rates, this step will not make you rich but every step adds to financial independence.

Overall CDs alone are not the answer but combined with other good choices, they are another valuable piece of the puzzle. The money is tucked away and it's too much of a pain to go get. And if others are asking to borrow it or use it, your hands are tied. You can't just go withdraw it. Financially secure people have a diversity of savings, investments, and wealth.

The whole reason I wanted to write this book was to help the average American. My family and I are just ordinary folks who get up each morning and head off to work. By no means am I where I'd like to be financially, but I want to help those of you who are where I once was. By the grace of God we have gone from having our house maxed out, along with our credit cards, and having a new car payment to now having the car paid off, zero dollars in credit card debt, only five years left on our mortgage, and gaining an emergency account. And we have opened up a Roth IRA, contributing more to our 401Ks, and made saving automatic.

Wherever you may be in life there is a way out, one step at a time and by putting one foot in front of the other. Rely on God for strength and encouragement. This is not an overnight transformation but a life changing journey. Begin to implement the money saving tips mentioned earlier and slowly see your future become brighter.

Investing

When it comes to investing I am by far not an expert, but I do know it is important to do so. Having a diversified portfolio is a must. The younger you get started, the higher your chance of becoming a millionaire will be. When my husband and I started investing, we had no idea of what we were doing and even how it all worked. We've come a long way baby! Now I check our investments monthly and have different investments with different companies.

Please don't misunderstand me—we are not millionaires. As a matter of fact not even close to having a net worth of a million dollars. We are regular, hard working people that have small investments. All six of us work hard and try our best. As you know from reading thus far, we have never really had a lot of spare money to invest until recently. As I write this I am still working two jobs, researching, and saving where I can.

First of all, if the company you work for offers a match program where they will contribute a percentage to your retirement account, without hesitation sign up. Take advantage of the benefits of your job. My teaching job does not offer any type of contribution matching, but I still opened a Roth IRA through a company set up for investing. My waitressing job offers a 401K matching program. It isn't a huge amount, but it still has helped out and over time will increase. In any event, begin investing.

Investing has been made easy. The investment companies have aggressive, moderate, and conservative portfolios to choose from. Usually the representative has you fill in a small questionnaire that will help the company decide what portfolio would be best for you. Once that is determined, you may start investing but always keep a sharp eye on your investments.

Prior to signing up you should do a little research on the company with whom you are going to be investing. This way you will be aware of the reputation of that company plus any annual fees. You should increase the percentage rate you are investing by at least 1% each year. So if you start at 10% of your pay, the next year increase that to 11% and continue that pattern. From experience I understand that is not always possible. Also keep in the mind the amount allotted yearly by the Federal Government for tax purposes. You are allowed to contribute up to $18,000 to a type of 401K and $5,500 to a Roth.

The key to investing is to leave your money in it to grow. If you take it out early, two major problems occur. Number one, you will lose 40% of your money right off the bat. There will be a 20% penalty slapped on the initial withdrawal and 20% tax that needs to be paid to Uncle Sam. Think about how hard you work for your money. Do you really want 40% of your money to fly right out the window? The next dilemma is very problematic. Are looking forward to retiring? I am as well. If you decide to dip in to your retirement early, it will postpone your retirement. So do not take your money out of your investments early at all costs.

Now there are situations that occur in life when you are forced to take money from your investments. For example at one point when we were financially strapped the most, we starting having problems with our septic system. It turned out that our leech field needed to be replaced. We couldn't borrow any more money from the bank and we have never asked our parents to help out. So there we were.

We did the last thing we wanted to do—we dipped into one of 401Ks and replaced our leech field. Talk about digging your hole deeper and making a bad situation worse. I've been there and have done that. Speaking from experience if at all possible leave your money alone and let it work for you. But in an emergency, it is sure good to have that to draw from.

Also make sure you don't put all your eggs in one basket so to speak. The stock market is very unpredictable and not always a reliable source of gain. If you are young, surfing the waves of the market is doable. Even if you are middle aged, you can ride out the waves. Past that point, your gains need to be part of your income. That is why I suggest other sources of investments.

Real Estate

When my husband was just 18 and I had recently turned 19, we ventured into a real estate agent's office. It was a moment in life I will not forget. To begin with, the agent thought we were an absolute joke at our age, but I had news for Mr. Funny Pants—we were buying a house.

The first few houses the agent showed us were more than mere fixer uppers; they were more like "time to call the demo team." At one of the beauties, the agent tried to explain the slanted floors were intentional to make it easier to walk to the garage. Talk about a joke! Now I am sure we didn't look like the most potential of customers, but we were there to make it happen. Needless to say after that adventure, we decided to go to a different real estate agency altogether. I do understand at our age we were considered questionable clients rather than prospective customers.

The next agency was super helpful and a pleasure to work with. However, the bank we were working with actually wanted a letter of explanation as to why at our age we had an interest in buying a house. I put my mind to work and my hands to action. I constructed that letter and we, as teenagers, were on our way to becoming homeowners. Owning a home is a great investment because it generally increases in value.

Remember an investment is defined as using your money for monetary gain. In other words, initially paying out some money with the expectation of gaining more in return. Real estate is another investment that has potential to make you great gains in a couple ways. Buying cheaper houses, renovating them, and then selling them is an excellent source of income.

Flipping houses has become very popular since the real estate market has hit such a decline. If you or your spouse possess skills that pertain to remodeling a home, the better the idea is for you. My husband is a carpenter by trade but is also capable of installing plumbing and wiring a house. He has the ability to build from the foundation up. He and I—well, mostly him—have done all of the renovations to our house. I have tried and tried to convince him to buy and flip a house up here, but he feels in this small town it would be hard to resell it. I hate to admit it but up here he may have a point. However, in more populated areas it is an excellent way to make more money.

Buying additional real estate as rental properties is like receiving another paycheck. Granted, like any investment it has an initial cost, but once the renters are in place you will be able to start paying off the property and then making extra money. Of course when setting the rental price, it's necessary to keep in mind that you need to have enough money in reserve for any repairs or improvements necessary. Another perk to this idea is years after you have bought the property and paid for it, you can sell it for absolute profit. On the other hand, you could keep the rental property for a retirement income. Either way it is a win, win situation.

If you have an emergency savings in place, all your debt paid off (including your mortgage), and you are investing in a

401K and a Roth IRA, then it's time to rise to the next challenge. I do advise you to make sure all of the other pieces are in place before you venture off into real estate investing (besides the house you live in). Without a solid foundation, what you worked so hard to complete could crumble down.

18

Future Glance

This next section of the book is devoted to the ones who are young, smart, and who will start off on the right foot. I only wish we had been in a position to set ourselves up for an easier journey with more secure financial status when we were young. The key word in this section is "plan." Obviously we, as humans, are unable to plan every aspect of our lives, but we are able to prepare for what we do know is ahead.

College Time

To those of you stay-at-home moms, bless your hearts. I cherish the time I had at home with my children. I was fortunate to stay home with all four of my children and only worked when we had serious financial stresses, like my husband breaking his leg, cutting three of his fingers off, and a shoulder operation. He has had some injuries that required lost time at work. Of course as time raced by, my husband's two jobs weren't cutting it for the six of us.

One summer afternoon I was sitting outside with the kids looking through the mail when I noticed a college schedule for the fall semester. I graduated from high school seven years earlier, but all of a sudden I had an intense feeling that I needed to go to college.

At that time in life we were four kids into this journey, and I was ready to mix it up and change our course. I told my husband I wanted to go to college for teaching. Well he chuckled and said, "Okay if you graduate and get a job, I will take you anywhere you would like to go in the United States." That was just more of an incentive for me. Thankfully through many crazy, long, tiring nights I did it, but guess what, he never took me to Hawaii. What a rip off! At some point I need to cash in on that promise. . .

When I made this decision, the handling of the details was pretty tricky. Remember I didn't have any family up this way except for my husband's side. Thankfully my mother-in-law watched my children when I was in class at the times my husband was working. She was great and I felt very comfortable leaving them with her. My mother-in-law was nervous about my new adventure. She wasn't quite sure that it would be the best decision for our family. As time went on, she finally came to realize that it was the right way to go.

When you first take a big step like this, there may be doubters but press on. Do not let people negatively influence you when you are trying to positively change your life to better you and your family. I had many who were skeptical that I could juggle four college classes, my house, and my four children. I will not deny it wasn't easy, and there were times I felt like throwing in the towel, but I didn't, and you can do it too.

Many people's lives consist of attending college, getting

married, and raising a family. Creating a quick sketch of the future will help you take the first step. The first biggie on the list is deciding what job you would like to start off with. There are two factors that could help you out here. Number one is a job that incorporates your strengths. The second factor needs to be to do what you enjoy doing. It certainly makes a difference if you enjoy getting up and heading off to work.

Once you have established what career you would like to pursue, it's time to decide what further education you need to make it happen. If you are lucky enough to have parents who have a college savings account in place for you, you are miles ahead of many in your shoes. If you are like a majority of us, you will have to seek higher education through means of loans, scholarships, and working hard. Either way, achieving the degree is what is important.

Deciding what university is best for your situation is of utmost importance. Carefully doing your research is critical. Numerous factors need to be considered—housing in that area, cost of living where it is located, and the availability of jobs for you are all vital components. The cost per credit hour at each college also has to be part of the equation. Keep in mind the degree you will hold is the same if you acquire at a state university or through a private college. The less debt you begin your career with, the better start you will have.

Along with the research on specific universities, you need to be aware of the average salary for the profession you are pursing. Knowing your approximate salary will let you know what wiggle room you have for college expenses. For example, my elected occupation, being a teacher, only yields an annual salary of $30,000 in Maine. For a four year degree, that isn't a lucrative income. So when I was college shopping, I leaned toward a college nearby that was the least expensive. But I chose a career that was very flexible for my family.

Always keep in mind that as long as you attend an accredited college, it's the degree that matters not the institution in which you accomplished the degree. State universities tend to cost less and offer you more financial aid. However, I can't emphasize enough to examine all the perks for any colleges that interest you. Finding the best college suited to you and your future profession is the ultimate goal.

Many times as high school students your kids work part time and are completely ecstatic about the income they're making. The experience I've had with my children is that when they first started earning money, it would burn holes in their pockets. They couldn't hold onto it for long. It opened up a world where they could buy extra items or head out to eat when they wanted to. At first I thought, *Why not their earning their own money, they don't have any bills, and they're still kids.*

As time went on and college arrived for my older children, it wasn't a good way of viewing my children working. With the first two, I had that mentality, but as the others approached college age, I changed the advice I gave them. I explained the importance of saving money no matter what. Have your children save a certain percentage of their income from day one. It will put both of you in a better position to go through the next step of life.

Purchasing a Home

Who hasn't pictured a sweet little home with a nice, white picket fence bordering the front yard? Due to the recession, buying a house has become a littler trickier than it used to be. As mentioned earlier under real estate, I understand situations that seem difficult or even out of reach.

My husband and I bought our first home as teenagers in the year 1992. It is quite an incredible story. We had a 10% down payment from stocks my deceased grandmother had left me. My husband had only been working a full time job for only six months and had recently graduated from high school. We had two children at this point in our lives. I was a stay at home teen mom. It would cost me more to pay someone to watch my two babies, ages almost two and six months old, than I would make working. It was a very precarious situation.

I had a dream before we originally were shown the house that this was the house for us to buy. God guides our path many times if we look for the direction from Him. "In all thy ways acknowledge Him and He shall direct they path" (Psalms 3:6). Shortly after we finished fixing up the necessary items on the house for the loan to be approved, we became homeowners as teenagers. Many banks today are not as willing to take chances on risky customers like we were. We were very blessed and I consider our house one of the many miracles God has granted me in my lifetime.

Where does this leave the current house hunters? Setting a budget and understanding what you and your spouse can afford is number one. When doing so, leave yourself a little wiggle room. It is so important to know what is allotted in your budget for housing.

One way to help you compute this is to think about your current rent. What you are paying now monthly helps you get a glimpse of what you will be able to afford. Keep in mind owning a house has some costs that renting does not. Also remember any repairs or problems are your responsibility. You are now the landlord so to speak. Therefore, make sure your house payment is less than your current rent. This leaves you with room to fix unexpected problems. Once you understand what you can afford, you are en route toward buying a new home.

Having ample money saved is an absolute must. Saving at least 20% of the cost of the home as a down payment is key. Many banks today will not even consider a mortgage application without the 20% down, although there are certain loans that will accept 10% down. Now along with the down payment, you need to think of other costs not pertaining to that. For example, closing costs, inspections costs, and other problems that may arise in the process need to be considered as well. To be on the safe side, if you have at least 30% of the cost of the home you would have your 20% for a down payment and then 10% to work with and plow through any unforeseen issues. If you are applying for a loan that accepts 10% down, you would only need 20% of the cost of the home. On top of that I would also have at least one month's payment set aside. Having this collected means you're ready to take the next step.

If you want to be a step ahead of the competition you

need to be pre-approved by a bank. It's not a huge process but it gives you some great leverage. Some agents will require you to be pre-approved before moving forward. In this neck of the woods, that is not common but is present in more populated areas. Along with bargaining power it lets you know, as a buyer, your limits. However, I would be cautious with your limit. It is not necessary to borrow the full amount. Take into account that everything you borrow will need to be paid back eventually and with interest tacked on. Borrowing to your full potential is not very wise and could strap you financially.

After that you are ready to find your house!

19

Mortgage Meltdown

There is a lot of conversation among the financial gurus on whether it is more beneficial to pay off your mortgage early or milk the loan for a tax break. With life experience and a lot of research, I believe paying off your mortgage is a win, win situation. Let's talk about why.

For starters, in order to receive the tax break, you need to itemize instead of taking the standard deduction. Now I do itemize, but you need to consider that the amount of interest you are paying a year needs to be less than what the deduction would gain you. I have a 2.99% interest rate on my mortgage, which is very low. As low as mine is, it still would save me more money to pay off my mortgage than use it as a deduction.

Another perk of paying a mortgage off is the money used to pay your mortgage could be put into savings or invested monthly. On top of saving or investing, paying off your mortgage early would free you from being strapped at your current job or would allow you to take a risk that could change your life for the better. I have wanted to own a bakery, and I am hoping in time that will happen for me, but for the moment I cannot take that risk. Once my mortgage is paid off, I will feel comfortable enough to pursue that dream.

There are a few simple steps that make it easier to whittle away at that mortgage. To begin with, when you first set up your mortgage, set it up in bi-weekly payments. Paying additional on the principal every month is also a smart money move. Making it automatic makes it painless. For example I out aside $320 a week for my mortgage, which is a bi-weekly payment of $511. That only totals up to $1,022 a month but I put $1280 in my checking account. Therefore I have an extra $250 a month to apply to the principal of my mortgage. Last but not least, take any sum of money you receive like a tax return or your annual raise and place that directly on your mortgage.

We all have a dream job that education, finances, or life in general keeps us from making a reality. I am a big advocate of continuing until you are victorious and that's my plan. As a side note I am only about five years away from paying off my mortgage, thank God! With a large mortgage payment, my ability to take risks, to gain my dream job, or early retirement is only a vision. But after paying off a mortgage, it is an achievable reality.

Refinancing for a Lower Interest Rate

Depending on your current interest rate, refinancing is one of the most effective ways to pay off your mortgage early. I won't ever forget the day I drove through the drive thru of our current lender and saw a large green sign that said, "Refinance Your Home with Us! At 2.99%." I thought that can't be right—2.99%? Well the only way for me to find out was to ask. So I inquired within the bank that very day.

Shortly after walking in, I sat down with a mortgage lender. Once I found out the details, and asked quite a few questions, we got the process going. He looked at me and questioned my husband not being present. I told him not to worry that he would be on board and he trusts me with the finances. With that being said, he proceeded. Of course that night I ran it by my husband and showed him the paperwork and that's when we started our refinance.

It was like on Black Friday when you wait in that freezing cold line to get in and grab that deal! That's how I felt that day. I knew this would save my family money monthly and bring us one step further to financial freedom.

Now with refinancing you need to take into account a few facts. In order for refinancing to be beneficial, it should be at least 2% different than your current interest rate. Here's why that is a factor. Whenever you do any type of loan, it costs money initially. You will have to pay for closing costs just like your first mortgage with the exceptions that the real estate agent and lawyer will not be part of the equation. Due to all the initial fees, you need that 2% to make the difference. In my case, the difference was 3% so I didn't have any hesitation in going forward.

Refinancing for a Shorter Term

Lessening the length of your mortgage term goes hand in hand with dropping the interest rate. Generally, the shorter the term of your loan, the less the interest rate will be. It will help you obtain a more preferable interest rate. Regardless of that, it will make the goal of paying off your mortgage more rapidly attainable.

When we refinanced, we changed our mortgage from a 20-year term to a 10-year term. Of course doing this increases the amount of money you will be paying out monthly for your mortgage. Our mortgage went up by $100 a month. We may have had to adjust our budget a bit, but it was well worth it. It's like running a race and shortening the distance you have to run by half—another huge step toward freeing you up from one of your biggest monthly debts.

Pay Additional on the Principle Monthly

A significant step in shortening the length of your mortgage is making additional principle payments on a monthly basis. When you establish the amount of your mortgage, the easiest way to be able to make principle payments is to budget the extra payment in your monthly amount. As I said earlier, my mortgage is $1,022 a month but I budget for $1,280. So at the end of the month I have $250 extra to put towards the principle of the loan.

In this day and age, making a principle payment is extremely easy. At the end of the month I go online and transfer $250 from my checking and apply it to the principle of the loan. In order to make sure I have adequate money to pay $1,250 on my mortgage monthly, I divide that amount by four weeks. So I save $320 a week in a checking account that is linked to my mortgage. If you do this from the start of your mortgage, you will view the extra money as a payment you owe rather than extra money you are collecting. We are by far creatures of habit! Make it a habit from the start, and it will become old hat.

When you are setting up your loan initially, it is best to have a checking account linked to your loan or mortgage. This will allow two events to happen easily. You will be able to have your mortgage payment automatically deducted from the account. Also, it will make it easy for you to make extra principle payments online by transferring the money between the linked accounts.

Do make sure when you are making the extra payments they are recorded as principle only. It is very important to ensure the extra payments are going strictly toward the principle balance of the loan. Usually online they give you choices in a drop down box like: regular payment, interest only payment, or principle only payment. I always double check which choice I picked. It is easy to click the wrong one, so thoroughly check over your choices. This process makes paying extra on the principle balance of your loan like a walk in the park on a sunny day.

Making Bi-weekly Payments

Another simple but super idea is making bi-weekly payments instead of monthly payments. This again does two things. One of the most prominent things that occurs is that you will make at least one extra payment a year. You may be thinking, *Well what good is that?* It's a huge help. Let me explain how. Just like making extra principle payments, making bi-weekly payments attack the principle, which in turn beats down the interest you are paying. Every little bit you pay toward the principle starts eating away at the loan, and in turn applies less money toward the interest. Think of this visual: you wouldn't open your window on a windy day and start throwing money out it. Well, that's what interest on a loan is—money out the window. Here's the other obvious help: you are making an extra payment each year by switching from monthly to bi-weekly. It is a wise move that has very little impact on your monthly budget.

If you having a deep desire to be debt free, your mortgage is an important factor to eliminate. Making an extra payment each year on top of monthly principle only payments and bi-weekly payments will just start devouring your mortgage. It is incredible to see it happen. As I explained earlier in this book, my husband and I just kept borrowing more and more money until we maxed out our house. I refinanced just 2½ years ago for a 10-year mortgage at 2.99%. With the advice I have given you, I have already shaved off almost four years from our mortgage. How do I know? It is very simple to check on your progress. There are many different mortgage calculators found online to check up on your progress.

You could also take your yearly tax return and apply it toward the principle of your loan. It's an excellent way to chop down the balance. We use our tax return to remodel and put some away for savings, but truthfully it is an awesome way to pay off your mortgage quicker.

20

Got to Give

As I am writing this, I am reminiscing about years ago when my husband and I had two small children, the third one on the way, barely paying the rent and hardly making ends meet. The church we were attending needed a new roof. On the spur of the moment, I decided to volunteer to give $200 toward the project. This was years ago and that seemed like $20,000 to us. We didn't have any money, not one single credit card, and no idea how I was going to get the money. I just knew that I was supposed to give that money and needed to do so.

Shortly after I volunteered the money, it arrived in various ways and to my surprise, we received more than I had pledged. At that point in my life, I was new to attending church and trying to understand God's ways. Since then I have attended church for years and I am still attempting to comprehend God's ways, but as the scripture says, "For my thoughts are not your thoughts, neither are your ways my ways, saith the Lord. For as the heavens are higher than the earth, so are my ways higher than your ways and my thoughts than your thoughts" (Isaiah 55 8-9).

It was so cool for me as a new Christian to obey God's

voice and see the rewards of doing so. It was a huge step of faith for me at that time. I can remember receiving a check in the mail from a doctor's office. It was deemed as an overpayment. The next day I went in to confirm that it was correct. The secretary said it was right and not to worry. That particular check covered the $200 I had pledged but more came my way! The blessings multiply when you give.

The point to the story is this it is an incredible blessing to give to others and charities. There is never any harm done when you help someone out, volunteer time at a shelter, or throw a little more in the offering plate. Only good comes from such actions. Better than the blessings here on earth is the account the God is taking for your deeds. "And let us not be weary in well doing: for in due season we shall reap, if you faint not. As we have therefore opportunity, let us do good unto all men especially unto the who are of the household of faith" (Galatians 6:9-10). You may not have your name up in lights, but your light has shone brightly in a dim place crying for hope.

Wherever you may be in life financially, there is someone worse off than you. Don't hesitate to help others. If it is cooking a small meal or baking a dessert for someone, it will make a difference, and you will be blessed. Bringing a smile to a neighbor's face or seeing a tear fall because of your kindness is worth any sacrifice made.

Helping others will positively change your life. Your situation will seem better and you'll feel joy that can be obtained no other way. Please know every act of kindness is noted. Your generosity may save someone's life, change it indefinitely, or create a lifelong friend. "Give and it shall be given unto to you: good measure, pressed down, and shaken together, and running over, shall men give unto your bosom. For with the same measure that ye mete withal it shall be measured to you again" (Luke 6:38).

Giving must be done from your heart. Give with love in mind not begrudgingly or because you feel you have to. All the perks of giving disappear if it is not done with a pure heart and good intentions. Remember, "And as ye would that men should do to you, do ye also to them likewise" (Luke 6:31). Treat others the way you would like to be treated. Giving and helping create a euphoria that cannot be replaced and an action that cannot be forgotten.

21

Repurpose, Reuse, Rejoice

Some of my fondest childhood memories include my brothers and I taking former machinery or other items and transforming them into masterpieces. We were famous for taking the push mower's motor and creating a pretty stellar go-kart, Crandall style. (That was my maiden name.) We spent hours building, constructing, and racing it down the road. I was the youngest of three children and the only girl so doing cool things like messing with machines was pretty neat. I was happy to be included in the project and even more ecstatic to race the baby.

Another way I save oodles of money today is to reuse and repurpose items. When I am redecorating a room, some of the former wall hangings or trinkets can be painted and used differently for the new room. I recently painted my den the new gray scheme that is so popular. I have a super cute wooden faith sign the kids had given me. It was brown, and the colors in the den are gray, white, black, and blue. So I grabbed a can of white spray paint and went to work. It took a couple of coats and now looks like it was built to dwell in my den.

Years ago when Wade and I didn't have much money and certainly not any to spare, we had to be creative in our renovations. My old kitchen needed some serious attention. A remodel was out of the question but a gallon of Kilz, sand paper, a gallon of paint, and some hands ready to get down and dirty were available. My daughter and I rolled up our sleeves and started a factory like remodel on the kitchen cabinets. One of us sanded and wiped them off. Then the other would paint them with Kilz, and lastly I slapped new color on. When the two coats were dry, we attached the old hardware and they looked brand new. New cabinets cost thousands of dollars, but painting them like I did only cost me less than a hundred.

The point in this chapter is before hitting the dump with that old item, think how you could use it if it were a different color or cleaned up. Honestly my girls' bureaus were painted each time I redid their rooms, or when they started looking shabby. It saved me a ton of money. Furniture is especially expensive so if you can make it last, you are way better off. Repurpose, reuse, and recycle while rejoicing about the money you are saving.

22

KEEP CLIMBING

Throughout my life, and I am sure yours as well, throwing in the towel looked much easier than facing the climb up the mountain. It brings me back to a field trip I had the opportunity to go on with my oldest daughter. We journeyed to Mount Katahdin to take a beautiful scenic hike. My friend and I were both chaperones, and I might add I was very young at the time. We let the kids decide whether we would take the extremely challenging route or the less challenging trail. Of course they wanted the harder one.

With sweat running down my beat red face, I kept trucking it. The kids were behind us, and we had to be an example and keep going. I can remember wondering how long the trail was and how much more of it was huge rocks in a vertical direction. Life is just like the hike I took. Your kids are watching how you face challenging situations. Do you take the road harder to travel but with a greater reward or stroll down easy street with less gain?

If there is anything I could convey to you is *do not give up!* It is so important that you continue to keep fighting for a better life for your family and yourself. Regardless of your situation or predicament, keep moving forward. Anyone who looked at my husband and me with three babies at age 19 and 20 would have shaken their head at us.

You *can* make your future better. Determination and hard work are two of the most important factors in changing any outcome. With God's help you can make the impossible possible. Take tiny steps until you're walking. Once you're walking, start speed walking, and then begin jogging. After jogging, run until you know you've made it for your family. After all we wake up each morning and head off to work for our family.

Each step won't be easy and there will be days and times when you're not sure how things will pan out, but somehow they do. I had many days when I was not sure what to do or how to do it. My older children remember the days when they had juice in their cereal because we just didn't have enough money for milk, but my children never went without food and by the grace of God have been very healthy. I can remember family members snickering at me when I decided to go to college with four small children. I heard questions like, "Are sure that is the best idea for your family?" Pursue what you know is right and what you know will help your family.

Each challenging journey has rough times and short-lived smooth sailing, but the outcome is worth the effort. Picking yourself up by the bootstraps won't be easy, but it will help your family. Keep going, keep fighting, keep working for a better life for you and your family.

My inspiration in life is God and my family. To battle and

conquer, you need a driving desire. Find a reason to dig your-self out. Give yourself goals and accomplish them. Never finish achieving; continue to strive and overcome. Encourage yourself to change your life for the better. Live each day just a little bit wiser than the day before. God bless and good luck.

About the Author

CATHY ESTABROOK resides in the small community of Houlton, Maine, with her husband and four children. She went through her teenage years with heavy responsibilities, having three of her four children by the time she was twenty.

Despite some challenges along the way, she accomplished a bachelor's degree in elementary education. After much research, effort, and growth, she has transformed her financial pitfalls into a bright fiscal future. Through many mistakes and vast experiences, she has destroyed the textbook theories of failure into soaring successes with God's guidance.

CPSIA information can be obtained
at www.ICGtesting.com
Printed in the USA
FSOW03n1301150617
35264FS